"One clarion call of the pandemic ___ rooms. In *Writing Clubs*, Patty a___ reimagine writing workshop where _____ as people and writers. They've anticipated all of our questions, and every chapter is chock-full of answers in the form of easy-to-use calendars, unit plans, schedules, mentor texts, and teacher talk. If you're looking for the future of writing workshop, it's right here."

— **Katie Cunningham**, author of *Start with Joy* and *Story*

"Too often when educators think about what their students need to flourish as writers, collaboration is not at the forefront of our minds. Well, no more! Lisa and Patty demonstrate the myriad ways collaboration is essential—not in the 'ask students to give feedback around checklist items' approach that is prevalent in classrooms, but as the heartbeat of students' writing lives. *Writing Clubs* is the book you didn't know you needed, but absolutely do. Lisa and Patty position the kind of collaboration that lives in writing clubs as vital; it is the pulse that propels writers forward and creates transformative writing experiences."

— **Sonja Cherry Paul**, educator, author, and cofounder #IREL, and **Dana Johansen**, middle school educator and author

"This book is written for teachers who wish to infuse new life into their writing workshop by implementing writing clubs that honor student choice and deepen classroom writing communities. Patty and Lisa have created a road map to help teachers implement complement and stand-alone writing clubs that will not only help students grow as writers, but will also help them learn how to collaborate. These are two life skills that will serve them well for the rest of their lives."

—**Stacey Shubitz**, author of *Welcome to Writing Workshop: Engaging Today's Students with a Model That Works*

Writing Clubs

Writing Clubs

Fostering Choice, Collaboration, and Community in the Writing Classroom

Lisa Eickholdt and Patricia Vitale-Reilly

Stenhouse
PUBLISHERS

www.stenhouse.com

PORTSMOUTH, NEW HAMPSHIRE

www.stenhouse.com

Library of Congress Cataloging-in-Publication Data
Names: Eickholdt, Lisa, author. | Vitale-Reilly, Patricia, author.
Title: Writing clubs : fostering choice, collaboration, and community in
   the writing classroom / Lisa Eickholdt and Patricia Vitale-Reilly.
Description: Portsmouth, New Hampshire : Stenhouse Publishers, 2021. |
   Includes bibliographical references and index. |
Identifiers: LCCN 2021027510 (print) | LCCN 2021027511 (ebook) | ISBN
   9781625313232 (paperback) | ISBN 9781625313249 (ebook)
Subjects: LCSH: Composition (Language arts)—Study and teaching (Secondary)
   | English language--Composition and exercises—Study and teaching
   (Secondary) | Mentor texts (Language arts)
Classification: LCC LB1631 .E48 2021 (print) | LCC LB1631 (ebook) | DDC
   428.0071/2—dc23
LC record available at https://lccn.loc.gov/2021027510
LC ebook record available at https://lccn.loc.gov/2021027511

Cover and interior design by Jill Shaffer
Typesetting by Eclipse Publishing Services

Printed in the United States of America

This book is printed on paper certified by third-party standards for sustainably managed forestry.

27 26 25 24 23 22 21   4371   9 8 7 6 5 4 3 2 1

To Keith and Jack,
members of my favorite club: our family.
—LE

To Kevin Reilly,
for our many years of love and laughter, and
for our two beautiful gifts: Rhiannon and Jack
—PVR

Contents

A Complete Table of Contents and Chapter Summaries

CHAPTER 1 An Introduction to Writing Clubs

In this chapter, we introduce the concept of writing clubs to teachers. We advocate for writing clubs by explaining how writing clubs can be an essential part of writing instruction, regardless of the approach or resources used. Standing on a variety of research to support writing collaborations—from Vygotsky's theory of more knowledgeable other (1978) to a recent survey of fifteen hundred of the world's CEOs (Palmisano 2010)—we unpack the "why" behind writing clubs and introduce teachers to a structure that can help their writers to thrive.

CHAPTER 2 Launching Writing Clubs: Building Community and Establishing Collaborations

The work of writing clubs begins through a simple and effective structure: the writing partnership. In this chapter, we demonstrate how to launch by building community and trust. We lay out partnerships as the stepping-stone to writing clubs and demonstrate how to create a collaborative structure that leads to successful writing clubs for students of all ages. We outline how you can incorporate writing clubs into a year of writing. We demonstrate how writing clubs fit into the workshop structure and can be an integral part of any unit of study, complementing that unit of study with the collaborative structure of clubs. We also show how you can use writing clubs as a stand-alone unit, providing teachers and students unique opportunities for collaborative units of study. Last, we show how writing clubs can be implemented in a variety of settings including a blended learning or hybrid model.

CHAPTER 3 Process Clubs: Using Clubs to Explore and Develop Process Skills

One of the most effective ways to collaborate around writing is to provide students with the opportunity to support each other across the writing process. In this chapter, we demonstrate how teachers can implement process clubs as an integral part of any unit of study. We show how students in writing clubs can provide feedback and support for each other as they move from brainstorming, to drafting, to revising, to editing, and finally to publishing.

CHAPTER 4 Craft Clubs: Studying Mentor Texts Together

In craft clubs, students study one craft technique through the work of various authors across texts. For example, one club might look across a set of picture books to see how different authors create an interesting lead or a satisfying ending. Another club might look across a set of texts to see how different authors use sensory images. In this chapter, we explain the important role mentor texts play in the writing process.

CHAPTER 5 Digital Clubs: Transforming Writing in Authentic Ways

In digital clubs, students explore various platforms. In this chapter, we demonstrate how teachers can implement digital clubs as an integral part of any unit of study. We show how to take students from exploration to creation as they take a genre piece and produce it in digital form. We show how this type of club can complement any type of writing, and how the genre of the unit can be paired with various digital forms including digital storybooks, book trailers, and multimedia poetry.

CHAPTER 6 Genre Clubs: Writing Our Favorite Kinds of Writing

Genre clubs are one of students' favorite stand-alone clubs because they allow them to compose texts they love, like graphic novels, comics, mysteries, poetry, picture books, and joke books. In this chapter, we explain how teachers can introduce genre clubs and support students as they study the characteristics unique to various types of texts.

CHAPTER 7 Author Clubs: Finding a Writing Mentor

A class favorite is the author club; students study the life of the writer, their office work (Ray 1999), and their craft. In this chapter, we demonstrate how to stand on the pillar of choice to engage students in the study of one club-chosen author. We provide teachers with a list of diverse authors that students can collaboratively study in order to emulate the moves and techniques of their chosen author.

CHAPTER 8 Conventions Clubs: Authentic Opportunities to Play with Writing

Conventions clubs are opportunities for students to discover and explore the power of conventions. During conventions clubs, students experiment and approximate, collaborate, and play with the rules of our language system. In this chapter, we show teachers how to support students in meaningful and authentic ways as they create opportunities for learning and growing with regard to building usage and style in writing.

Acknowledgments

Thank you to the many teachers and schools that we have had the pleasure of working in over the last three decades. In particular, Patty would like to thank the teachers in the Warwick Valley Central School District, with a special thank-you to Alisa Kadus, Maureen Wihry, Stacy Fitzgerald, and Jenn Disy, and the teachers in the Emerson Public Schools, with a special thank-you to April Catuogno and Brianna Peros. Lisa would like to thank the teachers in the Gwinnett County Public Schools, in particular Missy Renz, Mohana Nair, Genevieve Arhin, Jaleesa Pizarro, Meghan Smith, and Samantha Jenkins.

We also want to thank the entire Stenhouse team for helping us to bring writing clubs out into the world. A huge thank-you to Shannon St. Peter for her careful attention to every detail, to Mark Corsey of Eclipse Publishing Services for his project management, to Steph Levy for overseeing the project, to Pam Hunt for making our writing clear, and to Maureen Barbieri for believing in this project since day one!

Foreword

Paula Bourque, author of *Close Writing: Developing Purposeful Writers in Grades 2–6 and Spark! Quick Writes to Kindle Hearts and Minds in Elementary Classrooms*

Having just finished my thirty-fourth year of teaching, I feel as if I'm finishing my first. It is often said that change comes slowly to education, but those of us who had to reinvent our approaches to teaching during a global pandemic can file away that outdated maxim. As challenging as this COVID crisis has been for us, many colleagues have shared how this demanding experience has helped them focus more intentionally on what they value in their teaching and personal lives. We yearn for meaningful relationships, authentic learning experiences, and satisfying engagement for our students. We are emerging more committed to our convictions, and eager to put these priorities into practice. The timing and content of Lisa and Patty's book could not be better for us to support the rebuilding of our classroom communities with the powerful and purposeful instruction we thirst for.

This past year, while we practiced safe social distancing, we desperately missed intimate interactions and collaborative conversations. We realized their true value as we witnessed the effects of their absence on our students and the strength of our communities. *Writing Clubs* offers a potent pathway forward in reestablishing our priorities for collaboration, community, and choice in our writing classrooms.

In my book *Spark! Quick Writes to Kindle Hearts and Minds in Elementary Classrooms*, I share my belief in the importance of relationships in learning with *intradependence*, a model that I see embodied in Lisa and Patty's work. I wrote, "I see *intradependence* as a model that encourages working beside one another in our classrooms as mentors and resources to lift the independent learning goals of all. . . . We may not be collaborating on the same writing project or for a common outcome or grade, but we can support one another to grow personally, as well as collectively, as writers. When students mentor and teach one another, their confidence increases, as does the confidence of those learning from them." Writing clubs are the perfect approach for fostering intradependence in any classroom.

Since first reading Lisa's book *Learning from Classmates: Using Students' Writing as Mentor Texts,* I have seen the effectiveness of utilizing student mentors and mentor texts with peers, and it can be transformational. Students grow when they can lean on good writing that is within their own classrooms and their Zone of Proximal Development. They can imagine new ways of writing that are attainable with peer guidance. We hear comments such as "I can do that!" or "Oh, I want to try that!" that melt our writing teacher hearts!

I've facilitated book clubs in classrooms for years and have witnessed how those conversations can deepen reading comprehension and nurture a love for reading. Lisa and Patty's book helps us use this framework to elevate writing skills, social-emotional skills, and enjoyment in much the same way. Writing can be a lonely endeavor for many students. By embedding social supports and celebrations into our instruction, we can bring joy and jubilance into our writers' lives. We've observed this past year how much our students crave social interaction; let's tap into that natural desire to build engagement and strengthen our writing communities.

Finally, beyond a tragic pandemic, we have also seen the devastating impact on societies when people lack collaboration, compassion, and concern for one another. As a teacher, I am committed to raising the whole child and not just a writer or a reader. I want these children to grow into responsible and caring adults who can humanely navigate relationships and experiences. We can't just wish for it; we have to cultivate it with purpose and passion. This book is the right tool at the right time for that cultivation. Thank you, Lisa and Patty, for this labor of love. I hope it finds its way into the hearts and minds of teachers who are as committed to this collaboration as you are. It has found a home in my heart.

If you are still not sure, I invite you to use my sketchnote flowchart to help you decide if writing clubs are right for your classroom. I think you will find this as a helpful tool!

Section I

Laying the Foundation

Chapter 1

An Introduction to Writing Clubs

C ollaboration is all around us: It is apparent throughout history (Michelle and Barack Obama), in music, (Elton John and Bernie Taupin), and via innovation (Larry Page and Sergey Brin or Steve Jobs and Steve Wozniak).

In fact, a recent survey of CEOs determined that the number one skill they look for in future employees is the ability to collaborate (Palmisano 2010). However, in classrooms, our students don't often have these opportunities.

Therefore, it is essential that we provide multiple chances for them to learn in collaborative settings. In reading, our students learn and interact with peers in a variety of ways: through reading partnerships, reading centers, and reading or book clubs. In all reading collaborations, most especially in reading and book clubs, students can choose what they read, navigate the process and pacing of reading, talk with self-selected peers, and make decisions on how the reading impacts them, and how, in turn, they will impact the world with this knowledge.

Although all aspects of language arts—reading, writing, listening, and speaking—are intricately intertwined, the opportunity to collaborate as writers is dramatically untapped. That said, we believe collaborating is an essential and natural way to learn to become a better writer.

Real writers work in collaborative settings, as part of writing teams that "workshop" their writing frequently. They have their own professional posse—a group they go to when they most want to receive feedback and advice on their writing. So, too, should our students have these opportunities to work in authentic and engaging ways. In writing clubs, we envision a parallel experience to book clubs: students choose what they write, navigate the process and pacing of writing, talk with self-selected peers, and make decisions on how to impact the world with their voices and their words. Figure 1.1 illustrates this idea.

Figure 1.1
Tenets of Reading Clubs and Writing Clubs

Tenets of Reading Clubs	Tenets of Writing Clubs
Students:	Students:
• Choose what they read	• Choose what they write
• Navigate the process and pacing of reading	• Navigate the process and pacing of writing
• Talk with self-selected peers	• Talk with self-selected peers
• Make decisions on how the reading impacts them and how in turn they will impact the world with this knowledge	• Make decisions on how to impact the world with their voices and their words

As we have been implementing writing clubs in our own classrooms and the classrooms of others, one element we love about them is that writing clubs are authentic ways to read, write, speak, listen, and experiment with language use. Because writing clubs are a social construct, they provide students with the chance to interact powerfully and intentionally with the speaking and listening standards. In one unit, the teacher and students alike can explore all of the language arts and work to develop not only reading, writing, and language skills but also, more important, speaking and listening skills. Regardless of what state you teach in, metrics have been set for how students should interact with each other for the purposes of communication, presentation, and conversation. We can argue that these standards are among the most important in elementary education, because they are what our students need first as they move through their academic experience and transition to career and life. For example, the next-generation New York State anchor standards (NYS 2017), modeled after the CCSS (2010), expect the following.

COMPREHENSION AND COLLABORATION

STANDARD 1: Prepare for and participate effectively in a range of conversations and collaborations with diverse partners; express ideas clearly and persuasively, and build on those of others.

STANDARD 2: Integrate and evaluate information presented in diverse media and formats (including visual, quantitative, and oral).

STANDARD 3: Evaluate a speaker's point of view, reasoning, and use of evidence and rhetoric.

PRESENTATION OF KNOWLEDGE AND IDEAS

STANDARD 4: Present information, findings, and supporting evidence so that listeners can follow the line of reasoning. Ensure that the organization, development, and style are appropriate to the task, purpose, and audience.

STANDARD 5: Make strategic use of digital media and visual displays to express information and enhance understanding of presentations.

STANDARD 6: Adapt speech to a variety of contexts and communicative tasks, demonstrating command of academic English when indicated or appropriate.

Although these standards are specific to New York State, most state standards put forth similar metrics. We want students to participate in conversations with diverse partners, grow perspectives, utilize digital tools as forms of communication, and develop strategies for communicating ideas with, for, and to others. This book is grounded in these beliefs and provides students authentic ways to do this.

Writing can be a lonely endeavor. Even in workshop classrooms where students are surrounded by their peers, writing is generally completed alone. One way to combat the isolation of writing is through writing clubs. In writing clubs, students work with their peers to study areas of interest, such as a genre, an author, or a particular stage of the writing process, such as generating ideas or revising writing.

In classrooms that use clubs as an instructional approach, the teacher is not the only expert in the classroom; instead, she advocates for peer-to-peer learning by harnessing each student's expertise. Students are taught to look to their peers for help and as mentors. In writing club classrooms, every student's unique talents and strengths are recognized and used for the betterment of the group: creating a community based on mutual respect and admiration.

Another thing we love about writing clubs is how we are able to help students become more in tune with their own writing processes. We know that no one "right" writing process exists. Instead, many writers can exhibit moves as they write, and these moves are often called "*the writing process*" (Calkins 1994; Graves 1983). We also believe that every student's writing work is unique, fluid, and recursive. We encourage students to cycle through the processes of rehearsal, drafting, revising, and editing at their own pace and in their own way, so they can discover what works for them.

In addition to providing opportunities for students to collaborate, interact with the standards, and cultivate a process grounded in the idea of student as expert, writing clubs promote student choice. More than thirty years ago, Donald Murray encouraged teachers to create writing classrooms based on the work of real writers. He advocated for classroom communities where students collaborate and receive feedback from their peers and where students make many choices about their writing, including not only what to write about but also how to write it. Because writing clubs can be used within current genre studies or as their own stand-alone study, students can make key choices about their writing. When participating in clubs, students get to decide what they want to study, how they will study it, and what they will create with their writing.

We implement clubs in our writing classrooms in two ways. The first is within current writing units as a complement to students' ongoing work. The second is as a separate stand-alone unit. Let's take a closer look at both.

COMPLEMENT CLUBS

Writing clubs afford students the chance to give and receive feedback as they write. This feedback is an essential part of being a writer. Research by John Hattie into the effect size of various teaching practices (a quantitative measure of the extent of impact) found authentic feedback to be one of the most powerful forms of teaching with an effect size of .80 (Hattie 2009). Complement clubs enable teachers to provide time for students to receive peer feedback and support in authentic ways throughout the writing process.

Making Time for Complement Clubs

We make time for writing clubs within our current units by allowing time for students to meet with their clubs for ten–fifteen minutes during our writing block by borrowing time from independent writing and, often, extending club work into the share. Though any club can be done as a stand-alone unit, we prefer to do some club work as a supplement to current units. In this book, we discuss how process, craft, and digital clubs can be an accompaniment to current units of study. Writers benefit from learning how to support their peers with various strategies as they work through the writing process. They also benefit from examining various mentor texts in search of how a few key authors use specific craft techniques and from finding new ways to make traditional texts digital. Figure 1.2 shows how teachers can make time for writing clubs in their current writing workshops.

Figure 1.2
Incorporating Writing Clubs into Writing Workshop

Writing Workshop Block *without* Writing Clubs	Writing Workshop Block *with* Writing Clubs (Two or Three Days a Week)
1. Minilesson: 10 minutes	1. Minilesson: 10 minutes
2. Writing and Conferring: 30–40 minutes	2. Writing and Conferring: 25–30 minutes
3. Wrap-Up/Share: 5 minutes	3. Writing Clubs: 10–15 minutes
	4. Wrap-Up/Share: 5 minutes

In addition to envisioning how a writing workshop day with club time can go, consider how clubs can be incorporated into various units and where to place them in the year. Figure 1.3 shows an example of how clubs can be woven into a year of writing work.

Figure 1.3
A Sample Grade Four Writing Calendar with
Traditional Writing Units Supported with Complement Clubs

Time Frame and Timing	Unit
September (4 weeks)	Launch Unit (with process clubs)
October (4–6 weeks)	Personal Narrative
November/December (4 weeks)	Informational Writing (with craft clubs)
January (4 weeks)	Reviews
February/March (4–6 weeks)	Argument Writing
March/April (4–5 weeks)	Fiction
May/June (4–6 weeks)	Poetry (with digital clubs)

STAND-ALONE CLUBS

While working in writing classrooms across the country, we have noticed a change in recent years. In the past, students had many opportunities to choose not only what to write about but how they wanted to write it. In today's classrooms, we see many teachers moving from one genre study to the next, with no opportunities for students to choose their mode of writing. Moving from study to study across the year removes a key writing decision from students: What do I want to make of what I wrote?

Implementing stand-alone writing clubs allows students to choose their mode of writing and explore new aspects of composing. Students can form clubs around their favorite genres or authors, or to improve a characteristic of writing, such as word choice or conventions. Within these clubs, they support each other as they research, write, and publish various types of writing. Each type of club, whether genre, author, or conventions, affords students the opportunity to collaborate and make their own decisions about their writing work.

Making Time for Stand-Alone Clubs

We make time for stand-alone clubs by keeping a tight writing schedule: for the traditional units we teach each year, we allot four to five weeks per unit. This offers us plenty of time to incorporate several stand-alone clubs into our calendar. Figures 1.4 and 1.5 show sample writing calendars based on common units of study with time built in for some stand-alone writing clubs.

Figure 1.4
A Sample Grade Five Writing Calendar
That Incorporates Stand-Alone Writing Clubs

Time Frame and Timing	Unit
September (3 weeks)	Launch Unit
October (4 weeks)	Memoir: The Art of Telling Your Story
November (3–4 weeks)	Genre Clubs
December (2–3 weeks)	Convention Clubs
January (3–4 weeks)	Informational Writing
February/March (4–5 weeks)	Argument Writing: Literary Essay
April (3–4 weeks)	Poetry
May/June (4–5 weeks)	Author Clubs

Figure 1.5
A Sample Grade Six Writing Calendar That Incorporates
Stand-Alone Writing Clubs and Complement Clubs

Month	Unit of Study
October–mid-November	Launching the Year with the Personal Essay
January	Argument Writing with Conventions Clubs
March	Research Writing with Digital Clubs
May–June	Author Clubs (as a reading–writing unit)

Across the year, we need to offer students time to study all aspects of writing. This means we need to include opportunities for a closer examination of process and habits, craft, genre, and conventions. Using a club approach to teaching allows us to provide a more balanced writing curriculum across the year as we focus on each of these vital aspects. Figure 1.6 presents a menu of options that teachers might consider as they design their yearly calendar.

Figure 1.6
Yearly Calendar Options

Units in Process	Units in Genre	Units in Craft	Units in Conventions
Launching a Community of Writers	Making Our Voices Matter: A Study of Argument Writing	Author Study or Author Clubs (Chapter 7)	Conventions Clubs (Chapter 8)
Process Clubs (Chapter 3)	Writing to Teach: Informational Writing	Craft Clubs (Chapter 4)	
Audience Study	Telling My Story: A Study of Narrative Writing	Structure Study: Architects of Our Own Writing	
The End Is as Important as the Beginning: Yearly Reflections	Multigenre Clubs (Chapter 6)		
	Digital Clubs (Chapter 5)		

Although we have chosen to represent certain clubs as stand-alone or complement, most clubs are interchangeable. For example, conventions clubs make great stand-alone and complement clubs. Author and digital clubs are possible as stand-alone units, but both can also complement and support a unit of study as they provide a lens for collaboration and deeper study.

THE BASICS OF TEACHING WRITING CLUBS

In all our units, we present a way of working that is grounded in writing workshop. Workshop teaching is built around the idea that students should spend the bulk of their writing time practicing. Workshop has three main parts: a whole-group minilesson, a time for independent prac-

tice with conferring, and a whole-group wrap-up. We add a fourth component when we add clubs.

Workshop kicks off with students and teachers gathered in a meeting area for whole-group instruction or the minilesson. The minilesson is the time to address the needs of the class. Our goal is to teach short so that students can practice long. In our sample units, we begin the day with a minilesson.

After the minilesson, we send students away from the meeting area to find a spot to practice writing. Therefore, in workshop, students spend large amounts of time working on their writing and making decisions as writers. In our sample units, students will spend large chunks of time writing, but because this is a club unit (or a unit with club time), we may use some of this time for students to collaborate.

Workshop concludes with a final whole-group meeting. Often called "the share," this activity seems to be the neglected stepsister of workshop teaching. We like to think of the end of the workshop as a wrap-up rather than a share. When implementing writing clubs, and in our sample units, we may ask students to stay in their club or discuss club work as part of the wrap-up. This way, we preserve the writing time for writing yet have a perfect place for students to reflect and discuss the work they are doing in their clubs.

Materials Used in Writing Clubs

Four essential, go-to types of materials are used in writing clubs. They work in any unit and in any club or type of club (stand-alone or complement). These materials are:

- **Writer's Notebooks.** We believe that both teachers and students should have a writer's notebook! If you have a high-tech classroom or are teaching in a hybrid or remote model, and if your students operate well in Google Classroom or any other digital platform, you can use a digital writer's notebook. However, we prefer to use a paper notebook with student writers for the earlier parts of the writing process. Why? We have a few reasons, including that a paper notebook requires you to write longhand, something recent brain research supports as a more effective way for humans to process and retain information. In addition, we feel the paper notebook will enable more collaboration. Notebooks can be positioned between two writers; teachers can collect and read notebooks; students can hold, tab, and manipulate notebooks easily; and the tangible quality works for many writers. Once writers move into the drafting stage of the writing process, digital platforms can then be incorporated easily into the program.

Figure 1.7
Writer's Notebook

- **Anchor Charts and Other Visual Tools.** Anchor charts ground our teaching and provide a visual representation of the instruction from the unit. Done well, anchor charts are visual tools for writers to use both independently and collaboratively. We suggest that each unit of study have one to three anchor charts. We also suggest that anchor charts be colorful and visually appealing but not visually overstimulating. Less is more—never more than four or five items on the chart—so that all learners can access and use it. In addition, we value other visual tools such as a well-placed word wall, graphic or visual rubrics, and craft charts depicting authors, texts, and craft moves learned by the community.

I went to the beach with my family.

I went to the beach with my family. We went swimming and played in the waves.

I went to the beach with my family. It was a warm and sunny day. We went swimming and played in the waves.

I went to the beach with my family. It was a warm and sunny day. We went swimming and played in the waves. I said to my brother, "swimming is fun!"

Figure 1.8
Visual Rubric

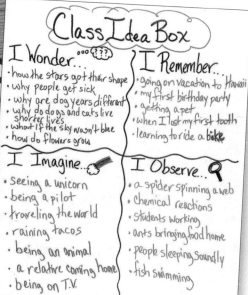

Figure 1.9
Anchor Chart

Class Idea Box

I Wonder... °°° ⟨???⟩
· how the stars got their shape
· why people get sick
· why are dog years different
· why do dogs and cats live shorter lives
· what if the sky wasn't blue
· how do flowers grow

I Remember...
· going on vacation to Hawaii
· my first birthday party
· getting a pet
· when I lost my first tooth
· learning to ride a bike

I Imagine... ✏
· seeing a unicorn
· being a pilot
· traveling the world
· raining tacos
· being an animal
· a relative coming home
· being on T.V.

I Observe... 🔍
· a spider spinning a web
· chemical reactions
· students working
· ants bringing food home
· people sleeping soundly
· fish swimming

- **Checklists.** Checklists are essential tools for student learning. They identify the success criteria (Hattie 2009) as well as provide a visual example of what a writer can and should be doing at any given time in the writing process. Our checklists follow the same rule as our anchor charts—never more than four or five items on it, so that it is accessible and well-utilized.

Writing Workshop Checklist

My plan for writing workshop is to:

☐ Start a new piece of writing.

☐ Go back and work on a piece of writing.

☐ Use our mentor texts to find ideas, inspirations, and craft moves.

☐ Have a writing conference.

How did my plan go? Rate how writing went for you today on a scale of 1-5.

1	2	3	4	5
Not well	Okay	Good	Great	Best Writing Workshop

Why?

_____

_____

What is my plan for our next writing workshop?

_____

_____

© Copyright Patricia Vitale-Reilly

Figure 1.10 Checklist

- **Writing Center with Other Pertinent Tools.** Although a writing center is typically thought of as a resource used in primary classrooms (K–2), we believe it should exist in all rooms and might include Chrome books; various types of paper to scaffold genre, process, and craft; pens of different colors (perhaps for different stages of the writing process); inspiring quotes from our favorite authors and eventually from the students in our classrooms; mentor texts; and various checklists to support students throughout the writing process.

Figure 1.11 Writing Center with Checklists

Considering Clubs in Blended, Hybrid, HyFlex, or Remote Learning

As we were in the final stages of drafting this book, COVID-19 took the world by storm, and as educators, we were expected to turn on a dime. Writing workshops pivoted to a remote format, and minilessons were either prerecorded videos or synchronous, live lessons taught over platforms such as Zoom or Google Meet. So what does that do to and for writing clubs?

As we also pivoted our work in classrooms with teachers, we began experimenting with teaching writing workshop in a remote setting, considering the ways students can collaborate with the use of technology or technological platforms. We learned so much and feel that this work actually *enhanced* rather than *detracted from* writing club work. Here is what we have learned:

1. Collaborations can occur in person, in synchronous online settings, and even in asynchronous online settings.

2. When in-person collaborations are a challenge, collaborating via a tech platform can be engaging, exciting, and safe!

3. Students need opportunities to collaborate and be together in the same "space" more than ever, and it is our role to figure out nontraditional ways to make this happen.

Where Can These Clubs Take Place?

Clubs can take place in multiple settings. First, clubs work in brick-and-mortar settings where the instruction and practice is in person. Teachers who look to incorporate technology in powerful and prominent ways will take that in-person setting and create a blended learning model. Other settings include a hybrid setting and its variation, the HyFlex hybrid setting. The last setting is the online setting where learning is remote and no in-person component is available to the learners. We further define these settings below.

■ **Blended Learning.** Blended learning takes place in a traditional, in-person brick-and-mortar setting. The teacher incorporates a heavy use of technology to implement direct instruction, conferring, small groups,

Figure 1.12 Online Learning Models and Writing Clubs

Model	Blended	Hybrid	Hyflex	Online Remote
Definition of the Model	Writing clubs in a blended classroom incorporate technology heavily for both instruction and practice.	Writing clubs are the perfect opportunity to envision engaging, effective, and safe collaborations. Students can be in a club with students from their hybrid cohort, meeting either in school on their in-person days or digitally on their remote days. The meetings on remote days can be synchronous (meeting in a Google or Zoom breakout room) or asynchronous ("meeting" on a platform that will allow for collaborations that do not happen in real time).	The HyFlex setting has been one of the more challenging teaching scenarios because the teacher is responsible for both the students in the cohort in front of them, as well as students in the cohort at home. HyFlex also presents a challenge to students because streaming in from a remote location is not as engaging and easy to participate in. Writing clubs can be an answer to this problem.	Writing clubs are a perfect activity to be part of a day of remote learning. One benefit of a remote setting is the ability to create asynchronous videos that students can watch at various times at their convenience.

continued on page 15

and other collaborations, as well as to create and store pertinent tools. An example would be flipping your writing workshop to deliver the mini-lesson online via a video to be viewed outside of class time so that the in-person time during the workshop can be used for student writing, differentiation, and collaboration.

■ **Hybrid Model.** A hybrid model is designed to take place partly in person and partly online. More traditionally, this model of instruction is used at the university level to offer students more flexibility and a variety of instructional settings and platforms. The "course" does not have to be

Model	Blended	Hybrid	Hyflex	Online Remote
Example of the Model in Action	Students watch videos, listen to read-aloud, or read print or digital examples related to their club. In addition, the teacher may flip the writing workshop so that the minilesson is watched prior to the workshop and the genre clubs have more time to meet and collaborate during the in-person workshop time.	Examples include using VoiceThread, speaking the noticings around their club, creating a Google Doc or placing a doc in Kami representing their club, and leaving a written comment or an audio or video comment with their noticings, feedback, or other ideas.	Teachers can create clubs across cohorts (two students in person are in a club with two students streaming in from a remote setting) or setting-based clubs. If the clubs cross settings, one advantage is that the in-person club members serve as a buddy to those at home, and collaborations serve as a scaffold to learning.	The teacher may choose to create a short video mini-lesson relating to each club instead of a whole-group minilesson. In particular, this approach would work well with author and genre clubs. It would also work well with a digital club because the teacher can meet with the club using their chosen platform.

divided 50/50 (in person to remote and online) but is designed to meet the needs of the students and the situation. In a hybrid model, students will have some in-person instruction as well as some online instruction that is typically delivered asynchronously. Examples of this asynchronous online instruction would include viewing lessons or presentations, reading course content, and collaborating with peers on a project or on an online learning platform. The idea behind hybrid instruction is the confluence between the in-person and online learning builds mastery. In the fall of 2020, many schools went to a hybrid model, with students in the school building on some days and learning from home on others, to deliver instruction safely while adhering to social distancing and CDC guidelines.

■ **HyFlex Model.** The HyFlex model is not the same as the hybrid model, but it does share common elements. This model was also created at the university level to attract students who needed more flexibility with course attendance. Students could choose to attend class in person or online, whichever best met their learning needs and lifestyle. In a HyFlex model, the online portion is structured as synchronous attendance with the class: the student is attending the class virtually, by streaming into the classroom via Zoom, Google Meet, or another platform. In the K–12 setting, some classrooms use HyFlex to meet the requirements of social distancing by allowing only some students to attend in person each day while the others "attend" by joining virtually. Just like in the hybrid model, the goal is that the in-person and online components of the teaching and learning work together to build student mastery.

■ **Online/Remote Learning.** Online learning in a remote setting is defined as a model where students do not attend in person—they attend school virtually. Typically an online "course" will combine synchronous (live) and asynchronous (not live) learning in a variety of ways. The spring of 2020 provided an example of this. Due to COVID-19, schools completely transitioned to an online model as each state and school district went into quarantine. At times, teachers met online with students in large and small groups to deliver live, synchronous instruction, and at other times, they created asynchronous videos and learning activities for students.

Figure 1.12 on pages 14–15 outlines how writing clubs work with the different online learning models. Look for information on implementing writing clubs in an online learning format in some club chapters.

NAVIGATING THIS BOOK

Regardless of the setting in which you teach, this book can be your guide to implementing a more joyful and student-centered approach to writing instruction. In Chapter 2, we define the way we have launched clubs not only in our classrooms but also in many of the hundreds of classrooms in which we have had the privilege to work. In the rest of the book, we dive into some of our favorite clubs. In Chapters 3, 4, and 5, we provide three examples of complement clubs. In Chapters 6, 7, and 8, we offer three examples of stand-alone clubs. Because we've found it helpful to break club work into a predictable structure, every club chapter is organized in the same way, and club work has three main parts. These parts include:

Part 1: Forming and Launching Clubs

Part 2: Lessons

Part 3: Clubbing Through the Unit

You may use this book in whatever way serves your purpose, but our hope is that once you have an idea of what a writing club is, you will dip in and out of the book to find a club that you want to implement and use that chapter as your springboard and muse for creating the kind of writing classroom that exemplifies what Don Graves stated in *Reflect, Reflect, Reflect* (Newkirk and Kittle, 2013, 215):

The process (of writing) must always be fresh to us and to children. The exciting thing about having the children teach us, and having us teach ourselves in our own writing, is that teaching becomes a process of discovery in its own right.

Chapter 2

Launching Writing Clubs: Building Community and Establishing Collaborations

I f you've ever written something and received feedback from another person, then you know the feeling of trepidation that comes with sharing your writing. Knowing another person will read your work and offer suggestions is an experience filled with risk. Many of us have had the misfortune of being on the receiving end of unhelpful or even seemingly spiteful comments about our writing—feedback such as "awk" or other "red pen" notes written in the margins of work we thought was good, or at least not "awkward," comes to mind. These negative experiences with feedback, though painful and definitely not constructive, are good for one thing: they have taught us how feedback should *not* go. One of the goals of writing clubs is to teach students to offer helpful feedback so that every child can become a confident and effective writer. This goal seems lofty—offering feedback that lifts the writer up and, at the same time, helps them grow can be challenging for teachers and students alike. Teaching students to offer thoughtful feedback doesn't happen overnight—it's a process, and one that requires us to teach kids two primary things: how to talk productively and respectfully to their peers and how to talk about writing.

TEACHING STUDENTS TO TALK TO PEERS

We love the new school year for many reasons: new books, new supplies, new faces. We also love the beginning of the year because it gives us something we feel we never have enough of—time! When we are launching our writing workshop at the start of a new school year, we have time to teach students how to talk about text and how to talk to their peers. We have more time because our students may not be able to write for the entire writing workshop. We allot forty-five to sixty minutes a day for writing workshop, with our kids writing for thirty to forty minutes of that time. At the beginning of the term, though, many students don't have the stamina to write for that long yet, so we take advantage of the extra time and use it to lay the foundation for a year of collaboration. This collaboration begins by making students feel safe and part of a writing community.

Building a Classroom Community

Creating a classroom community is one the most vital aspects of teaching. No matter how sound our pedagogy or how well-crafted our techniques, if students don't feel like they are part of a group, learning will not occur (Petersen 1992). A feeling of community creates an environment where students feel safe to take risks in their writing (and all other learning). Routman (1999, 20) writes, "We need to respect the diversity, culture, and language of our students' families. By valuing students' language, experiences, and background—for example, by encouraging them to tell the stories of their lives . . . we blur the boundaries between home and school and make school part of life as a place for relevant learning." As Routman suggests, a powerful way to foster a culture of respect and trust is to encourage students to share their stories, so we get to know each other as people. Some of the ways we get to know our students include:

- **Read-Alouds.** One of our favorite ways to help students get to know one another is by reading aloud. Sharing beautiful picture books, poetry, and current events about common human experiences evokes memories of similar experiences in children, memories they want to share. After the read-aloud, we share the memories the book triggered for us. When we share our stories and humorous anecdotes about family and friends, students open up. Talk soon fills the room as partners and small groups organically form around shared experiences. Through storytelling, we learn we are more alike than different. Figure 2.1 shows a list of some of our favorite books we like to read at the beginning of the year.

Figure 2.1
Favorite Read-Alouds for the Beginning of the Year

I Walk with Vanessa by Kerascoet
All Are Welcome by Alexander Penfold and Suzanne Kaufmann
All the Places to Love by Patricia MacLachlan and Mike Wimmer
Roller Coaster by Marla Frazee
Fireflies by Julie Brinckloe
Woman Hollering Creek by Sandra Cisneros
Those Shoes by Maribeth Boelts and Noah Jones
The Invisible Boy by Trudy Ludwig and Patrice Barton
Each Kindness by Jacqueline Woodson
The Day You Begin by Jacqueline Woodson
Pink Is for Boys by Rob Pearlman and Eda Kaban
Last Stop on Market Street by Matt de la Peña
Love by Matt de la Peña
Be Kind by Pat Zietlow Miller
Woke: A Young Poet's Call to Justice by Mahogany L. Brown with Elizabeth Acevedo and Olivia Gatwood
We Rise We Resist We Raise Our Voices edited by Wade Hudson and Cheryl Willis Hudson
Word After Word After Word by Patricia MacLachlan
Flying Lessons & Other Stories edited by Ellen Oh

The other way that we build community and prepare students to work in powerful and productive collaborations is to engage them in writing exercises that enable us to get to know them and, more important, let them get to know one another. The following are our favorite ways to build community in a writing classroom:

- **Six-Word Memoirs.** Another way we invite students to reveal themselves is through very short stories or six-word memoirs. Legend has it that Ernest Hemingway was once challenged to write a full story in six words. Hemingway famously responded with: "For Sale: baby shoes, never worn." In 2006, *Smith* magazine asked readers to reenact the challenge. Readers responded in droves, and the Six-Word Memoir project was born (http://www.smithmag .net/sixwordbook/about/). We show students examples of six-word memoirs from *Smith*'s Teen site (https://www.sixwordmemoirs .com/teens/) and let them create their own on sentence strips that we post in the room. Kids love writing and sharing these with one another and the world via the hashtag #SixWordStories. A couple of six-word memoirs Lisa has shared with her students include: Get off Twitter and get writing!; Life's too short for uncomfortable shoes.

- **Humans of New York.** Literacy teacher extraordinaire, Jessica Lifshitz (@Jess5th), taught us to harness the power of human interest stories by imitating the famous Humans of New York (HONY) website (www.humansofnewyork.com). The HONY project includes photographs and brief stories about the inhabitants of New York City. The site, which has more than twenty million followers, provides readers around the world with a daily glimpse into the lives of local New Yorkers. For the Humans of Room 16 project, Jess takes photos of her students and asks them to write short stories about themselves to share with their peers. She then posts photos and stories in her room and shares them digitally with parents. Figure 2.2 shows an example of one student's HONY story.

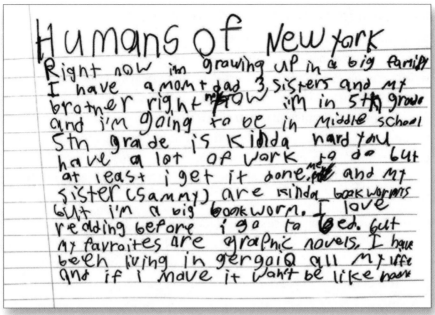

Figure 2.2 HONY Story

- **Heart Maps.** Famed author and poet Georgia Heard taught us all the power of sharing what we love. Heart maps, which began as a way to help students generate ideas for their poetry, have become a worldwide phenomenon and prompted Heard to write a book devoted solely to the topic. When creating a heart map, students are asked to consider what they love or what lives inside their heart and "map" it. The results are a beautiful and colorful representation of what really matters to each child. Visit the hashtag #HeartMaps on Twitter for some examples.

Getting to Know Each Other as Writers

As we're creating a community where students know each other as people, we are also beginning to learn about each other as writers. This process is a surefire way to prepare students for powerful partner and club work. We implement two structures to practice this at the beginning of the year: introducing feedback structures during the share time and creating expert lists.

Introducing Feedback During the Share Time

Regardless of the approach you use for writing, one common structure of many approaches is a share session or wrap-up at the end of the writing time. The share is powerful in many ways because it provides time to reflect, acknowledge, reiterate, and share. For us, this time is ideal for introducing feedback structures that will enable students to get to know one another as writers and will move students toward writing collaborations. One of our favorites is a structure that one of Patty's classes once called, "Sitting in the Chair" (Graves and Hansen 1983). It goes like this:

- Each day one writer sits in the feedback chair. In Patty's classroom, this was just the chair that Patty typically sat in during minilessons. Here, she gave the chair to a writer in the class, and she joined the rest of the writers in the meeting area.

- The writer asks the community to give feedback on a part of their writing. We limit the selection to be either one sentence or one paragraph because we want to fit this practice into the typical timing of the share—between five and ten minutes. The writer asks for specific feedback (Does my lead engage you as a reader? Can you follow the dialogue in this scene? Does my word choice pack a punch?) and then reads the part. To assist less experienced writers, and for Patty's students at the beginning of the year, the class generated a list of ways to ask for feedback in your writing. See the sample class chart in Figure 2.3. Or, you can simply provide writers with two general yet powerful ways to ask for feedback: Does this part make sense? Does this part interest you as a reader?

- Students listened to the writer and then implemented a simple feedback structure called "glow and a grow." A "glow" is a compliment about what a writer is doing well, and a "grow" is constructive feedback. Through this activity, each writer learns to ask for and take in feedback as well as how to provide feedback that is positive and powerful.

Figure 2.3
Feedback Chart

Ways to Ask for Feedback on Our Writing
Consider *what part* of your writing you want feedback on: • Lead • Ending • Organization/transitions • Specific element: body paragraph, craft element, dialogue, etc.
Start with a *phrase*: • Does this part make sense? • Can you help me with _____? • Can we look at _____? • Does this part interest you as a reader?

Creating Expert Lists

We've also found it helpful to begin by seeking out each child's strengths and creating an expert list of them (Vitale-Reilly 2017). We use our writing workshop time to talk with kids about their writing and observe them working with peers. As we informally assess our students, we are looking for what they are good at. We take note when a student has lots of ideas in their writing notebook and inquire about how they accomplished it. We share their response with the rest of the class and add "idea

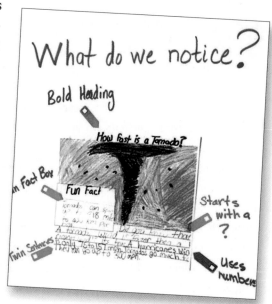

Figure 2.4
Annotated Student
Mentor Text Chart

generation" under their name on our expert chart. We notice when a student finds a unique way to plan and add "planning" under their name on the list. We pay attention to the students others seek out for assistance with spelling or illustrating as well. Conferring with an eye toward what students can do and ways they can mentor each other creates a culture of respect. It also conveys an important idea to students: everyone in this classroom has something worthy to offer (Eickholdt 2015). Figures 2.4 and 2.5 show examples of how we build on students' strengths in our classrooms. To further facilitate students' knowledge of their peers as writers, we also allow time for lots of partner work.

> Do you need help with paragraphing in your story? Sign below to meet with Trinity during workshop.
>
> 1. _____
> 2. _____
> 3. _____
> 4. _____
> 5. _____
> 6. _____

Figure 2.5
Sign-up Sheet for
Peer-led Lesson

The Power of Partnerships

Now that we have established some whole-class structures and ways to get to know each other as people and as writers, we are ready to begin collaborations. Also during this beginning-of-the-year unit, where we launch our community of writers, we introduce partnerships. We don't officially partner students up at first. Instead, we make sure every child has the opportunity to partner with every other student in the class at least once. Patty calls this speed partnering (Vitale-Reilly 2017). The goal is for students to have the opportunity to collaborate and talk with everyone, even for just five to ten minutes. We provide partner opportunities throughout our workshop: we ask students to partner during the minilesson and work together, to partner during writing to make plans and share ideas, and to partner at the end of writing to share their writing. After each partnership experience, we ask students to jot down one positive thing about their partner or the experience in their notebooks to refer to later. Speed partnering shows students that every child has unique qualities that may make them a good fit as a partner. We keep track of this speed dating on a grid so we can be sure each child has had the opportunity to work with everyone in the class.

Establishing Long-Term Partnerships

As students partner up, we observe and take notes. We notice who works well together and who does not; who is a "talker" and who is more of a listener. We also pay attention to how students interact across the day:

Who plays together at recess? Who shares books during reading? Who do kids sit next to at lunch? After a few weeks of partnering in workshop, we ask students to look back at their notes and list several students they'd like to work with for a while (writing partners are long term, usually throughout the duration of a unit, but not for the entire year). We then use students' requests, our notes from observations, and information from the class expert list to create what we hope will be the first of many well-matched collaborations throughout the year.

TEACHING STUDENTS TO TALK DEEPLY ABOUT WRITING

Peer feedback is an important part of writing (Graves 1983), so we jump into it early in the year, using the share as an entry point to this important skill. Although we work with students on sentence stems and provide guided practice on how to offer helpful advice to fellow writers, providing feedback is tough, and initially many students aren't effective at it. In our work, we've noticed ineffective peer feedback often comes in two primary ways: nonspecific praise or editing. Nonspecific praise often sounds something like, "I like your story." or "Your beginning was good."

These comments, though well intended, are not helpful to the writer. Hearing that someone likes your story or parts of it without learning what they enjoyed and why doesn't help the writer recreate the move in future pieces of writing. When students do try to move away from compliments and give constructive feedback, they often take on the role of a copy editor and attempt to correct spelling, punctuation, and grammar errors. Though we believe students must edit their writing, and peer editing can be helpful when students are ready to publish, our goal for writing clubs is for feedback regarding the content of each student's writing—feedback that helps students learn more about how to be a better writer. Teaching students to move away from unhelpful praise and editing comments and provide meaningful feedback begins by teaching them how to notice and talk with specificity about the craft of writing.

Reading Like Writers

When writers read, they study text as an insider (Ray 1999). This insider's perspective is necessary when you are trying to get better at something. Lisa's husband has coached high school football for more than twenty-five years and is a student of the game. What Keith sees as he watches football is very different from what most people see. When the quarterback gets sacked, we all notice. But as a defensive line coach, Keith also notices how the lineman got to the quarterback. He pays close attention to the move the lineman uses to beat his opponent. Does he use a swim, rip, or spin technique to make the play? (Lisa's knowledge of football terms should be impressive to you at this point.) As a coach, Keith doesn't only pay attention to the play, he notices how the player executed it. Keith watches football as an insider, so he can improve his coaching. This is how we want our writers to look at a text. Like all of us, writers notice a beautiful piece; the difference is they also pay attention to how the author created that beauty.

Noticing Writing Craft

Noticing writing craft begins with teaching students to pay attention to their reactions while they read. When we feel happy, sad, or mad while reading a text, it's because the author did something to make us feel this way. We teach students to pay attention to when they feel strongly and then ask them to make a theory about the writing move. We do this work together first so students can do it later on their own and with their partners. Let's look at an example of how this plays out in the classroom.

It's late September in a fifth-grade classroom. Lisa is teaching students the first of many lessons on studying mentor texts. She read the lovely piece, "Eleven," by Sandra Cisneros to them earlier as a read-aloud, and she is now using it in her minilesson to model how to notice and name the craft in the writing (Calkins and Marron 2013). Lisa displays the text on a document camera for all the kids to see and gives each child a copy to keep in their writing folders. The lesson begins.

Lisa: Writers, today we're going to study the beautiful piece of mentor text, "Eleven," that we read yesterday. A mentor is someone you look up to: often it's someone who teaches you how to do something. A mentor text is a piece of writing that, when you study it, can help you learn how to be a better writer.

To use a mentor text as a model, we need to pay attention to our thinking as we read and notice the parts that make us feel strongly: happy, mad, sad, or angry. When we notice these parts, we need to stop and think about what the writer did to make us feel so strongly.

Writers use certain techniques, or moves, as they write. Writers call these moves *craft*.

Let me show you what I mean. I'm going to read "Eleven" aloud again and pay attention to my thinking, so I can notice and name the craft in Sandra Cisneros's writing. Watch me now.

Lisa reads the text and pauses at the part where the teacher puts the ugly sweater on her desk.

Lisa: Wow, I am going to stop here. This part is standing out to me. Let's read it again.

"*That's not, I don't, You're not . . . Not mine," I finally say in a little voice that was me when I was like four.*

"Of course it's yours," Mrs. Price says, "I remember you wearing it once." Because she's older and the teacher, she's right and I'm not.

This part stands out to me because it makes me feel ashamed and frustrated. I can tell the girl is embarrassed by the ugly old sweater with the long jump-rope arms, and she's trying to tell her teacher that's it's not hers, but the teacher won't listen. I can tell she feels helpless—like she's a small child who nobody listens to.

But why does this part stand out to me? What is the writer doing here? Hmmm . . . I think this part stands out to me because of the talking.

We all know talking is an important way to build a scene and bring characters to life, but what is it about this talking here that's making me feel so strongly? Hmmm . . . I think it's because of the way the girl is talking—the way she's stuttering when she says, "That's not, I don't, You're not . . . Not mine . . ."

The way the author made her character talk in that halting way shows me that she has so much more to say, but she's too afraid to talk back to her teacher. I know that sometimes when I'm nervous or upset, I get tongue tied and can't make my thoughts come out correctly. I think the girl feels the same way here.

The author also wrote that she said it in a voice that was hers "when she was like four." I think this part stood out to me because the writer showed how the character was feeling by changing the way she spoke into a nervous way and describing how her voice as that of a small child.

Wow . . . so powerful. Sandra Cisneros just taught me that it's not just *what* the character says but *how* they say it—so important.

Did you notice how I paid attention to my thinking as I read, pausing when I found a part where I felt strongly, and then I thought about what the writer did to make me feel that way? That's one way writers study the craft in a mentor text.

Let's keep reading and see if we can find other parts.

Lisa continues reading and pauses a few sentences down when she gets to the part that states, "Not mine, not mine, not mine . . ."

Lisa: Okay, I'm going to stop again. This part stands out to me because I'm getting frustrated. The girl repeats this phrase, "Not mine, not mine, not mine . . ." here, and we know she says it again a few sentences down. *(Hands shoot up around the classroom and kids start commenting that they notice the words in other places. They begin excitedly pointing out various places in the text where they see the words* not *and* mine.*)*

Oh, I see you all are dying to add to the conversation. Look at your copy with your partner, and see where else you notice these words. Then think about why they are standing out to us.

The kids turn and talk with their writing partners, pointing out the many times in the text they see the words repeated. The class then discusses how the words *not* and *mine* are woven throughout the piece.

Lisa: Come back to me. I was listening in as you worked with your partners. You all found a few other times these words were in the story, so we notice the writer is repeating these words. And I think that it's this repetition that makes us feel her frustration. Casey and her partner noticed something else. Girls, share what you observed.

Casey: She never actually says the words aloud. She just repeats them to herself, like she's talking in her mind.

Lisa: Great observation! So not only are the words repeated to emphasize their importance, but the girl never actually says them aloud, only in her mind. This part stands out to us because the phrase is repeated throughout the text and also because of the way the character says them only to herself. It's like she's screaming in her mind, but nobody can hear. How frustrating! One way Sandra Cisneros conveys the character's insistence that the ugly, old sweater isn't hers is through repetition. Interesting writing technique—repetition can be a very powerful move.

Thumbs up if you think you might try either one of these craft moves we just observed—either describing how a character spoke or using repetition to convey emotion in your writing. *(Most students put their thumbs up.)*

I'm going to add those moves to our anchor chart to help us all remember them.

Okay, now it's your turn. I want you and your partner to keep reading, pause when you notice you have a strong feeling, and then consider what the writer did to make you feel that way. Then, we'll come back together and talk.

Lisa uses predictable language as she noticed the writing moves in Sandra Cisneros's writing. This is by design. When Lisa models her observations, she begins with the phrase, "This part stands out to me because . . ." Then she moves to considering the craft behind the move and names it by stating, "I think it stands out to me because the writer . . ." When she turns it over to the students, they use the same sentence stems to find parts that stand out to them and theorize why. Lisa posts these sentence stems and the steps for studying text for positive qualities on a chart in the room, so students can refer back to it as they practice reading like writers with other mentor texts and their classmates' writing. Figure 2.6 shows the chart that hangs in the classroom.

Figure 2.6
Steps to Reading Like a Writer

Steps to Reading Like a Writer
Notice: Pay attention to your thoughts as you read. Pause when you feel strongly: happy, sad, mad, frustrated, or embarrassed.
Say, "This part stands out to me because . . ."
Name: Consider what the writer did to make you feel this way.
Say, "I think it stands out to me because the writer . . ."

The previous lesson is an example of the many on studying mentor texts that we will teach across the year. We begin by asking students to notice when they feel strongly and pause to consider what the writer did to create that emotion. As the year progresses, we continue to study mentor texts in our minilessons. Soon, we ask students to also pay attention to parts that evoke strong images and parts that stand out because they like them for some reason. Studying text in this way teaches students how to be a better partner because they can find and name the craft moves in their partner's writing. It has the added benefit of teaching them powerful writing techniques to use in their own writing.

Giving Your Partner a "Glow"

After students have spent time studying text with us, we ask them to practice noticing and naming the positive attributes in their partner's writing. We have already introduced this into the share session, so students have had guided practice with providing feedback, but we know they need more work. We continue our glow and grow protocol and ask students to first provide a glow, or specific praise, to their partners each day. We ask students to use the same language we used in our work together when we studied mentor text, stating, "This part stands out to me because . . ." and "I think this stands out to me because you . . ." Once students are successful at praising their partner's writing, we can move to teaching them how to respond in a constructive way.

Providing Effective Feedback in Writing

To enhance our students' ability to offer feedback, we ask students to listen to a piece and notice when they have a question, want to know more, or wish the writer had used a certain writing strategy. We use our own writing in feedback lessons so we can create pieces that mimic the kinds of writing we see kids doing in class. In the following example, Lisa uses her writing as a demonstration text. You'll notice her piece lacks development. She wrote this sparse piece because she noticed many of her kids were writing in such a way, and because she wanted to be sure there were lots of opportunities for kids to offer suggestions on how to improve her writing. Let's take a look at her lesson.

Lisa: Writers, we've been learning how to study text and name techniques writers use to make their writing more interesting. It's important to find the beauty in writing and point it out. It helps the author be aware of what they did, and it also helps the reader learn new strategies to make their writing better. In addition to finding all the great things in your partner's writing, you can also help them by offering feedback. Giving someone feedback means that we listen to their writing and try to suggest some things they might do to make it better—easier to envision, to understand, or more powerful.

Today I'm going to teach you how to offer suggestions to a writer using a piece I wrote. Let me show you what I mean. I'm going to read my piece aloud, and as I read it, I want you to listen closely and pay attention to your thinking. I want you to notice when you have a question, when you want to know more about something, or when you wished I would have used a writing strategy because you think it would have made my writing better. *(She jots the things to think about on a chart.)* When you notice any of those things, jot a quick note to yourself. Questions? *(She pauses and answers a few questions.)*

Thumbs up if you're ready. Okay, let's begin.

> *One sunny day I went to the park with Keith and Jack. Jack had just learned to ride a two-wheeler and was excited to go show off his new skills. Keith and I were glad to be outside together on such a beautiful day.*
>
> *When we got to the park, Keith unpacked all the bikes. I helped Jack get on his helmet, and we put on ours. We headed to the trail. Jack quickly pedaled ahead of us, and we smiled as we he zoomed out of sight and rounded the corner.*
>
> *When we got to the corner, I began to worry. I couldn't see Jack any longer, but I could see a big hill. Jack had only just learned to ride a two-wheeler, and not falling while biking down a hill would be tough for him. I began to pedal faster as I searched for him. I yelled for him. I was really worried now. My hands were sweating as I gripped the handlebars tight.*
>
> *Keith began yelling and pedaling quickly, too. We reached the bottom of the hill and looked both ways. Still no Jack. I was afraid he was laying on the ground someplace hurt. I pedaled around the corner and finally saw a head of blond hair. He was*

*fine after all! He had done it! I was so happy I caught up to him
and gave him a big hug.*

That's what I have so far. Please take a minute to finish your
notes. Turn and share what you're thinking about my writing with
your partner. How can you offer me some feedback on what I
wrote? Do you have questions or suggestions for me? If I were your
writing partner, what advice would you offer me? *(She waits while
kids turn and talk and compare ideas.)*

I see you made some notes, Elizabeth and Mira. Do you have
some suggestions for me?

Elizabeth: Yes. The part where you said you thought your son had
fallen down the hill.

Lisa: Yes, in the third paragraph of my piece. Let me put a copy up
here for us to look at.

Elizabeth: Yeah, we both noticed that in that part you told us a
little bit about what you were thinking. You said you were worried
a couple times and your hands were sweaty. Those parts stood out
to us because we could tell you were worried.

Lisa: Thanks.

Elizabeth: But we thought it would make your piece stronger if
you told us more thinking there. Like you said you were worried,
but you know how we learned to talk to ourselves? Maybe you
could talk to yourself there a little bit like we learned from Sandra
Cisneros.

Lisa: Oh, I see. So, you're saying I could use some internal dialogue
to show how upset I was when I couldn't find Jack?

Elizabeth and Mira: Yes!

Lisa: Good suggestion. I'll keep that in mind when I revise. I'll
make a note here in the margins of my piece. Thanks!

Anyone else? *(Hands shoot up across the carpet.)*

Let's hear what Ben and Dylan have to say.

Ben and Dylan: We like your story, but we thought it would be better if you added more talking, too. You know how you always say talking brings your characters to life? Well, your characters aren't very alive.

Lisa: Ha! Good point. So, you think my characters are kind of flat, and your suggestion is to liven them up with some talking. Where do you think I need to add more dialogue?

Ben: Umm, like, everywhere. (Everyone laughs) You don't have any. You kind of do when you said you were yelling but not really.

Lisa: You're right! That really isn't talking. Talking would be when I say the words that came out of my mouth. I just said I yelled. It would be better to actually make my character yell, wouldn't it? I hadn't noticed I lacked dialogue. I'll keep that in mind when I go back to this piece *(makes a note at the top of her piece)*. So far we've had two suggestions to make my writing better. Does anyone have a question about the piece?

Adrian: I was wondering something. How did your son make it down the hill without falling?

Lisa: Good question. He told me that when he saw the hill, he got off his bike and jogged it down the hill. Pretty clever, actually. Do you think I should add that part?

Adrian: Yes, because I was wondering how he didn't fall.

Lisa: I think you're right. I'll remember to add more details later *(jots a note next to that part in her story)*. Writers, today we learned how to give someone feedback to make their writing better. You listened closely as I read my piece to you. You paid attention to your thinking and took notes. Then, you kindly offered me suggestions about how to improve my piece or asked me a question when you were wondering something. This is another way you can help someone be a better writer. We're going to practice this with my writing a few times. Soon I'll ask you to try it with your partner. I also want you to try this on your own: read your piece aloud to yourself, and monitor your thinking. When you notice one of these items on the chart, stop and think about how you can change your writing to answer a question or add more information to make it better. That's what writers do: they reread their writing with a critical eye. Got it? Okay, let's get to work!

In Lisa's minilesson, she asked students to go through the same process they will go through when they offer feedback, or a grow, to their partner and later when they do this in their clubs. Teaching students to pay attention to their thinking and ask a question or offer a suggestion is a simple way to provide feedback. You will notice there was no talk of conventions in Lisa's lesson. When teaching kids to offer suggestions to others, we make it clear that they are not allowed to comment on things such as spelling, grammar, and punctuation. They are not editors—we want feedback on content, not conventions. To facilitate this work, we have found it helpful to ask students to listen without looking at the writing. After students practice giving feedback as a group on a few of the teacher's pieces, we ask them to use the same protocol with their partner. Figure 2.7 shows an anchor chart with the steps to providing a glow and a grow.

Figure 2.7
Providing a Glow and a Grow

Writer	Partner

1. The writer states what she wants help with in her writing. For example, "Can you help me with my lead?"
 	
2. The writer reads the relevant part of the piece.
 	
3. The writer listens (and notes) the partner's suggestion(s) and commits to trying something in their writing.
	1. The partner listens to the writer's question.
	
	2. The partner listens and/or reads along, considering what the writer wants help with but also noticing what they like and what the writer did well.
	
	3. The partner gives the writer:
	  a. A compliment noting something the writer did well (Glow)
	  b. A suggestion based on the writer's request (Grow)

MOVING TO CLUBS

Our kids will continue to hone their feedback skills with their partners during our launch unit, and then, once our first genre-based unit is under way, we form clubs. To create clubs, we ask one partnership to join another partnership, creating a group of four students. The clubs are purposefully kept to two partnerships to allow students to continue working with their partners on days their club doesn't meet. (Clubs generally meet two days a week.) We also keep clubs small because having fewer students in a group promotes more social interaction. When clubs meet, we want to ensure every child is an active participant, either sharing their writing or offering feedback. If a club contains too many students, some might become disengaged or wander off task.

Clubs are built on the bedrock of partner work. Therefore, like partnerships, clubs require a protocol for providing feedback. During each club meeting, two members of the group are scheduled to read their writing and receive feedback. To prepare for their meeting, the author who is sharing finds a part in their piece that needs some work. In our minilessons on feedback, we model for kids how to read their pieces aloud and place a sticky next to a part that isn't working for them in some way: it's not conveying what they intend, it doesn't sound quite right, or they just don't like it. As the author reads, the other members actively listen and offer suggestions. We work with the group to create a protocol for giving and receiving feedback in clubs, and post the steps in the room. Figure 2.8 shows an example of a club protocol.

Figure 2.8
Writing Club Feedback Protocol

Writer	Club
• The author states what she wants help with in her writing. For example, "Does my lead work?" • The author reads the section aloud to the group.	• The club echoes the writer's request for feedback. • The members listen and jot notes (if needed).

Club	Writer
• Every member takes turns offering feedback.	• The author listens, responds, and makes notes on their piece.
• After the author considers the feedback, club members consider whether something offered to this writer would work in their own piece.	• The author chooses how to use the feedback. Club protocol is that the author commits to *trying* one suggestion in their piece.

LAYING THE GROUNDWORK FOR WRITING CLUBS

The work we did in this chapter has helped students build a writing community that values every student as a person and a writer. It has helped us begin teaching students how to talk to their peers in a constructive manner and how to talk in an informed way about writing techniques. Teaching students how to talk to peers and how to talk about text has laid the foundation for creating successful writing clubs throughout the year. In upcoming chapters, we will discuss how to make time for clubs throughout the year and how to implement various writing clubs.

Complement Clubs

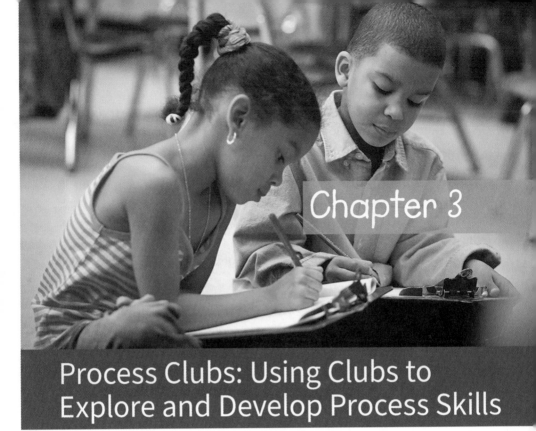

Chapter 3

Process Clubs: Using Clubs to Explore and Develop Process Skills

I t is early in the school year, and workshop is finally starting to have that working hum—less herding cats, more organized chaos—but Patty can tell her students are in a writing workshop rhythm and flow. Engagement is high, and her students really love to write—something that should not be taken for granted. As she takes a minute to glance around the room, clipboard with kid-watching notes in hand, she celebrates this accomplishment: students have the structure down, and she has managed to implement the minilesson in about ten minutes. She knows the next step is to move students through the writing process, but she also knows that doing so is no easy task.

The writing process is the heartbeat of writing. If there is anything we want students to take away from their year with us, it is the writing process. But . . . what is writing process? For us, the writing process is what Donald Murray, in *The Leaflet,* described as the three main stages of writing.

The writing process itself can be divided into three stages: prewriting, writing, and rewriting. The amount of time a writer spends in each stage depends on his personality, his work habits, his maturity as a craftsman, and the challenge of what he is trying to say. It is not a rigid lock-step process, but most writers most of the time pass through these three stages. (1972)

Prewriting, writing, rewriting . . . hmmm, yes, that has always made sense to Patty. Even when she is firing off a quick text or writing a "honey-do" list on the fridge, she moves through that process, albeit quickly. So, where does this leave Patty and her students, and how does this affect what they will be focused on during the next few weeks of the school year? This we believe:

- A writing process is as essential to a writer as air is to humans.

- Although the process has three main stages, writers move fluidly and individually through the writing process.

- The beginning of the year is the place not only to explore the writing process with students but also to establish structures and routines that will guide the time and bind the day.

- Writers learn by doing.

- The writing process, like all elements of writing, is not a solitary act. Writers are individuals, who must explore the writing process in their own way (Murray 1972), but writers also collaborate. Students work best in what Murray describes as a "context of shared success. Those who write well are teaching themselves, each other, and the teacher how writing is made effective" (1989, 25).

And that leads Patty to want to teach this writing process, not just through a series of minilessons, or through a series of days where writers are living recursively through the process, but in a way that is collaborative, a way that creates authentic opportunities to work with peers who mentor each other. This setting is where writing clubs are born.

PREPARING FOR PROCESS CLUBS

Before jumping into process clubs, we have to do a few things to ensure this club runs smoothly.

Figure 3.1
Writing Process Chart

Gathering Materials

Process clubs, like most clubs, don't require a complex set of additional materials. As students are clubbing through a unit and through the writing process, they will be using the materials they typically use during writing time (outlined in Chapter 1, Figures 1.7–1.10). For us, those materials are a writer's notebook (print or digital), anchor charts and other digital tools, and materials for collaboration and publishing.

The only other tool we like to use in process clubs are writing process charts, which we see as essential. These charts can exist in many forms (vertical, showing steps, circular, showing recursiveness, horizontal, showing parts to a process). Regardless of the form, a visual of the process is helpful, not only for times when writers are in process clubs but throughout any writing workshop. We make these charts interactive. Anchor charts can inadvertently become wallpaper, sometimes even visually overstimulating, so we think carefully about what is already on display and how we will use the new chart. We add sticky notes, clips, and magnets to display student names, so that students can identify and demonstrate where they are in the writing process in any unit of study.

Envisioning How the Work Will Go

Like anything else, process clubs are a field of dreams: "If you build it, they will come." Therefore, we believe it is helpful to envision where clubs will fit into the unit and how long the clubs will run.

When Will Clubs Happen?

In Chapter 1, we provided options for how writing clubs can fit into the existing fabric of writing time. Writing clubs are part of the writing workshop, borrowing time from the independent practice and share. What some find confusing about writing workshop is how students spend their writing time. Writers certainly practice what is taught in the minilesson, but they do not spend the entire time doing just that. For example, if the minilesson is about choosing paper that matches your writing for the day, it wouldn't take the entire independent practice time—it would take (at most) three to five minutes. Students would then be working on their writing, composing texts, and making decisions for the remainder of the writing time. The same is true for any type of minilesson. For example, if we teach writers to add dialogue to a narrative piece, they would not necessarily spend the next thirty-five minutes doing this. We call this concept the practice percentage rule (Vitale-Reilly 2015), and in general, it is around a 25 percent:75 percent ratio. In other words, students spend about 25 percent of the writing time working on the day's minilesson teaching point but 75 percent of the time on their actual writing, working on various texts, trying out new and previously taught strategies, collaborating with other writers, and in essence, making decisions as writers. These decisions may include:

- **Topic Choice.** The idea I will write about.

- **Task Choice.** Starting a new piece/entry, going back to writing.

- **Workspace Choice.** Where in the room I do my writing. We often refer to this as a student's "smart spot"—a place where they can be their best writing selves.

- **Craft Choice.** What moves I incorporate as a writer.

This means that in a writing workshop, students are off in various places, making decisions about the pieces they are composing, writing about self-selected topics. This affair is usually not an "anything goes" situation but rather a bracketed choice ruled by the unit. A unit of study typically lasts four to five weeks and is often focused on a specific genre. For example, in a third-grade classroom, students may be engaged in a study of nonfiction articles. The teacher's minilessons are about the genre, craft, and form of nonfiction feature articles. During the writing time, students compose numerous entries about self-selected topics of expertise. When writing these texts, they use the features and genre elements they have learned, collaborate with other writers, and apply this learning in writing that aims to teach readers about these topics. In another example, seventh-grade students may embark on a study of how to write historical fiction texts. The focus of this unit is explicit in the teacher's minilessons as she teaches students strategies to help them read, understand, emulate, and compose historical fiction. It will also be apparent in the students' practice as they rehearse, draft, revise, collaborate, and edit this type of text. If this is the paradigm of our teaching, then peer collaborations have a natural place in the learning, and complement clubs can fit into *any* unit of study.

As an example, envision the third-grade feature article unit. The minilesson (in process, genre, craft, and structure of nonfiction articles) occurs during the first ten minutes. The independent practice takes place for the next thirty minutes. Twice a week, process clubs meet, and students support each other with process skills (stamina, engagement, topic choice, reading like a writer) and through the writing process (rehearsal, draft, revise, edit, publish). The last five minutes of the writing workshop is the wrap-up.

Setting an Ending Date

If process clubs are a complement to a unit of study, then the time allotted for them varies depending on the unit. As a general rule of thumb, we typically launch the writing unit first, and a few days to a week later, we launch process clubs as part of that unit. For example, with the third-grade feature articles, we would launch the unit, spending the first few days immersing our students in the genre and trying on topics for size, and then launch the process clubs. (See specific examples in the next section, Teaching Points to Consider, and in the section titled Lessons.) This enables our students to benefit from collaborations across the writing process: prewriting (rehearsal, thinking about topics, generating topic ideas, try-it writing), writing (drafting), and rewriting (revision, editing). In this unit, clubs would last for about three out of the five weeks of the unit.

Teaching Points to Consider

We suggest opening up the curriculum to include lessons in process—not just *the writing process* but also other processes that are essential to writers as they build the habits and routines of effective writers. With the third-grade feature article unit, the teacher usually teaches lessons that pertain to that genre (genre elements and text features, research, structuring an article, developing writing through facts, anecdotes, quotes, comparisons, and various text features) but also teaches lessons that develop the writing process and provide writers with strategies to work on with classmates in writing clubs. These lessons apply to all writers, in any unit, in all clubs. Examples of possible process lessons in any unit where complement process clubs are used are shown in Figure 3.2.

Figure 3.2
Possible Process Club Minilessons: Habits of Good Writers

	Lesson Topic	Lesson Prompts
Process Category: Habits of Good Writers	**Stamina**	Strong writers write longer, stronger, and at a consistent pace. Do you notice when you do that? I do, so today, I am going to teach you how to build your writing stamina by writing longer and at a consistent pace.
		Strong writers write longer, stronger, and at a consistent pace. Writing partners can support this by helping you to set goals, make plans, and check in on progress. Today, I will teach you how to set partnership stamina goals.
	Finding Writing Ideas	Writers use four lenses for idea building: wonder, remember, observe, imagine. Today, I am going to teach you how you can . . . (wonder, remember, observe, imagine) to find writing ideas.
		Writers often reread their writing notebooks to find writing ideas. It is like digging through buried treasure in a goldmine—the gold is there! Today, I am going to teach you how to reread your writing notebook like an archaeologist looking for buried treasure.

	Lesson Topic	Lesson Prompts
Process Category: Habits of Good Writers	**Finding Writing Ideas** (continued)	Writers find ideas in their everyday lives. One way to capture these ideas is to . . . (map your heart, create a map of writing territories, list your favorite people, places, objects). Today, I am going to teach you how to . . .
	Developing Writing	All parts of a story are important, but in a narrative, the most important part is called the heart of the story. It is the part that most illuminates what the writer really wants to say. It is important to stretch that part out and slow down the action by including the inside story—feelings and thoughts.
		We have been talking about how writers stretch writing, but they also do the opposite—narrow down their writing by narrowing the topic. Today, I am going to teach you how to go from a large topic—a watermelon—to a small moment topic—a seed. See Figure 3.3 for an anchor chart of this generating strategy.
		Even when I am generating entries in a notebook, I want to develop my writing so that I say what I want to say in the way I want to say it. For me, I use strategies that help me develop my writing by getting to an important part and elaborating. Today, I am going to teach you how to use the strategy . . . (write across pages, lift a line, use a memory window, etc.) to develop your writing.
	Being an Engaged Writer with a Strong Identity	Strong writers know who they are as writers; they have a strong writing identity. One way to know your writing identity is to know your identity as a person. Today, I am going to teach you how to write a six-word memoir that shows who you are as a person and a writer.
		Writers have a strong identity when they know who they are as a writer. They can name qualities they have and qualities they strive for. Today, I am going to teach you how to examine yourself as a writer to find and name those qualities.
	Using Checklists	Many of you have commented that I have these small pieces of paper with lists on them, and that often I have check marks or other marks next to the items in the list. As I have explained, those are my checklists. I use them in other areas of my life, but I also use them in writing. Checklists help writers to remember what it is that they want to include in their writing. Today, I am going to teach you how to use a checklist.

Figure 3.2 (continued)
Possible Process Club Minilessons: Habits of Good Writers

Lesson Topic	Lesson Prompts
Using Checklists (continued)	The most common question I get asked as a teacher is whether I think the writer is finished with their writing. Although I always encourage a writer to reach out to me for advice and support, the fact is that only the writer can decide if the writing feels complete. Today, I am going to teach you how to use a checklist to determine if your writing piece is finished.
Setting Goals	Writers, like all people, work on their craft by setting goals. But a goal without a plan is just a lofty aspiration. Today, I am going to teach you how to set a goal and create a plan that will help you achieve that goal.
	Do you have a writer you admire? Someone who you would love to write just like? I do, and it is one way I work to set goals. Today, I am going to teach you how to look at writing from a writer you admire and use your admiration to set goals.

Process Category: Habits of Good Writers

Figure 3.3
Anchor Chart of a Process Strategy Taught as a Minilesson and Practiced in Process Clubs

Figure 3.4
Possible Process Club Minilessons: Collaborations

	Lesson Topic	Lesson Prompts
Process Category: Collaborations	**Utilizing Writing Partners in the Writing Process**	Writing partners help their fellow writer generate writing ideas, but they also help them across the writing process. When partners are helping each other after they have written something, they want to make sure they tell their partner what is working well in the writing and what their partner can work on. Today, I am going to teach you how you can give your partner a glow—something they did well—and a grow—something they can work on.
	Utilizing Writing Partners to Build Engagement and Identity	Yesterday, we created a class glow and grow chart to document our strengths and goals as writers. This work will go smoothly if we find a writer to celebrate these strengths and work toward the goals. Today, I am going to teach you how to find a writer in our community who can help you celebrate your strengths and work toward your goals.
	Providing Feedback to Collaborators	Put your thumb up if you have ever been told how to do something, or how to do something better, by a teacher, friend, or even well-meaning acquaintance? Keep your thumb up if you did not like getting that feedback. I have felt the same way. It is important to provide your writing partner/club member with feedback that is helpful to them and said in a way they can "hear" it. Today, I am going to teach you a simple three-step process using our writing feedback chart for giving other writers suggestions.
	Working with Multiple Writers in Clubs	Some of you have mentioned that you like the way we do morning meeting: we have steps that we follow and parts we do each day. Well, writing clubs work best when each club has protocols—a way the club is run so that every member feels comfortable and confident in the steps you follow and the parts you do each club meeting. Today, I am going to teach you how to create club protocols that you and your club will love.
		Club members don't just support writing; they support each other—their goals and plans as writers. One way to support a club member with a goal is to be an active part of their plan. Today, I am going to teach you how to support your club members with their writing goals.

Figure 3.5
Possible Process Club Minilessons: The Writing Process

Process Category: The Writing Process

Lesson Topic	Lesson Prompts
Rehearsal	Writing appears to be a solitary act, but it is in fact a collaborative endeavor. The best writers have other writers with whom they collaborate. Today, I am going to teach you how to utilize your writing club to rehearse writing ideas.
Drafting	Drafting can be hard if you sit down and try to get words down on a blank page. Just like in all other parts of the writing process, writers have a go-to strategy for drafting. Today, I am going to teach you how to . . . (talk it out, use storytelling, narrow your topic, plan in the margins, create an idea box, make a memory window, draft an outline) as a strategy for drafting.
	We have learned a lot of strategies this year, but the key to strategies is knowing when and how to use them. It's not a question of a strategy being right or wrong; it is more about matching the strategy to the writer and to the purpose. Today, I am going to teach you how to dip into your strategy toolbox and choose a drafting strategy that matches you, the writer, and your task and purpose, the writing.
Revisiting/ Revising	Sometimes writing comes quickly and painlessly and is a one and done—one time writing and the entry I wrote is all I have to say. But many times, writing doesn't go that way, and our best writing comes when we revisit old entries and explore what else we have to say. Today, I am going to teach you how to revisit a piece of writing and continue writing that entry.
	I know how good it feels when we finish a draft. We feel like we are done! But good writers revise. *Revision* is a word that literally means to resee or to see again. Today, I am going to teach you how to go back to your writing, resee what you have written, and make changes that will be clearer or more inviting to your reader.
	Revision can feel hard, but you make only two main moves when you revise: you add or you take out. How do you know what to do? You need to go back to your writing and ask yourself: Is this enough? Is this too much or not connected? Today, I am going to teach you how to go back to your writing and revise it by asking: Is this too much or not connected to my big idea?

Lesson Topic	Lesson Prompts
Using a Writer's Tools	All artists have special tools that are part of their discipline, and writers are no different. We have writing tools in this room that support us as writers. Today, I am going to teach you how to use our writing tools across the writing process.
	We have been exploring the tools that a writer has, and although all tools are important, the most important tool is the writer's notebook. It is important to use your writer's notebook as a tool for writing, and one way you can do that is to use it as a . . . (generating tool for ideas, tool to remind yourself of strategies you have learned, tool that contains pearls of good writing that can mentor you, etc.). Today, I am going to teach you how to use a writer's notebook as a . . .
Editing as a Process	Have you ever tried to read something that was hard to read because the writing contained many errors? I have, and boy is it tough! Writers don't always get their writing completely correct the first time that they write. I know this happens to me because I am just trying to get my ideas down. So, we want to be sure we take time to make our writing conventionally correct. Today, I am going to teach you how to go back to writing to edit for the big three: spelling, punctuation, and capitalization.

Process Category: The Writing Process

If the process club is a complement to the launching writing unit of study, we tend to position the clubs to support idea generating (finding ideas, developing ideas), collaborations (how to use a partner or club), and/ or the writing process (rehearsal strategies, drafting, revising, editing).

If the process club is a complement to any other unit of study in the year, we vary the process lesson within the unit to support the development of process skills that this particular class needs. In the third-grade feature article unit, a teacher might choose to spiral back to collaboration lessons on providing feedback to members of a club or introduce a stamina minilesson that enables club members to support the amount of time they can write and the development of words they can put on the page. From there, the focus will be on club support through certain stages of the writing process.

CLUB TIME

Adding a complement club layer to any unit of study is an exciting step to take. Collaboration adds a lens of engagement that brings the writing to new heights.

Part One: Forming and Launching Clubs

As complement clubs are integrated into an existing unit, they can be implemented during the entire unit or just for part of the time. Therefore, we will want to let students know of this exciting feature to their upcoming or current unit of study.

Day One: The Big Reveal

We have launched process clubs in many classrooms, and the first day is always an exciting one. It is especially thrilling in classrooms where students value their writing partners, understand the purpose and function of feedback, and are excited to work alongside other students! Here is an example from a recent process club that Patty launched in Mrs. Murray's fifth-grade classroom.

Patty: Friends, I realize Mrs. Murray let you know via a Google Classroom announcement that your current memoir unit will have an exciting feature added this week. I know you all loved the riddle she created to reveal what was to come:

"What uses mentor texts, writers' notebooks, and checklists, is part of writing time, and consists of you and three writing friends?"

Well, a writing club, of course! We will be adding this component to our unit next week.

Of course, this group of fifth-grade writers was incredibly excited at the thought of this new venture. Because this was the second unit of the year, and because Mrs. Murray took time in the launch unit to teach the writing process and introduce partnerships and a feedback protocol, her writers were ready and eager for a more substantial collaboration.

This announcement let students know that there would be a twist on their narrative unit—something they were more than ready for, having studied narrative writing since kindergarten. Patty took the lead in the conversation and began by asking students to define what it means to be in a club. She then asked students to name the process skills they wanted to develop further, as well as the ways they hoped their club might support them. The conversation went something like this:

Patty: Writers: today is an exciting day! I know that many of you have been asking Mrs. Murray about this new component to the memoir unit, and we have been a little vague about it. Well, we are going to add a new layer to the memoir unit— writing clubs to help you support each other throughout the process.

Looking around the room, she could see that students were excited, but they had questions.

Patty continued: During the launch of our writing unit, we learned that it is vital that each writer knows themselves as a writer. This means not only having a strong writing identity but also having a good sense of the writing process. We have seen the power of partnerships—a writing colleague who can support you as you move through the writing process. Today, we are going to take the power of two and turn it into the power of four and pair up two partnerships to create a writing club.

We then asked students to turn and talk with their partners to discuss what excites them most about writing clubs. We then asked them to share their questions:

- Who will be in each club? Can they have some say in forming the clubs?

- What will the clubs do? Will they have set meeting times like in reading clubs, or can they get together whenever they feel they need to?

- Can they still meet with just their partner?
- How will writing time be different? Or, will it be mostly the same?

Patty responded: All good questions, friends, and here is what we are thinking:

- We hoped that you would want to have some say in forming clubs. So today, you will have some time to meet with your partner and discuss two things: What do you think you can most offer a club? And what support would you want from your club? We will take a look at your answers and pair up partnerships.

- Clubs will operate in similar ways to partnerships but with more voices and more time to collaborate. This means we will have a club element in the rest of the unit of study. Specifically, the clubs will analyze mentor texts together and find a personal club favorite, use club members to rehearse writing—this can include talking out ideas or making decisions about topics—and provide feedback to drafts using our glow and grow protocol.

- We will have set times for clubs, but we are also happy to allow clubs to meet, if they feel the need, beyond that time. We will all have to keep an eye on stamina, remember our adage of "never a day without a line," and keep up our writing. And yes, you can still meet with your partner outside of club time if you feel a one-to-one conference is best for you. Just let club members know.

- And last, writing time will be almost the same as always, with some minor adjustments to the time. We will want to meet with clubs about twice a week, and we will borrow time from both the writing time and the wrap-up. We'll post a schedule for you to see.

One Classroom's Journey

Teachers can allow partners to get together to meet to discuss the two questions on that first day (as Patty and Mrs. Murray did) or have them talk the next day. Again, partners should be asked to explore and discuss two important questions:

1. What do you think you can most offer a club?

2. What support do you want from your club?

Partners in this class had really thoughtful conversations, offering insight to what students felt they could share with others, as well as what purpose they wanted the club to serve. They shared the following ideas:

- **Jared and Tomo:** Jared and I are very different writers, with strengths in different parts of the writing process: Tomo, generating topics; Jared, rethinking leads. But we both have issues with being  clear in our writing. We know what we want to say, but sometimes we don't say it in a way that others can understand and "see and feel" our stories. We would like to find club members who can help with that.

- **Naomi and Rishon:** Naomi and I are alike as writers, and we both LOVE *The House on Mango Street* and Sandra Cisneros. We would love to be in a club with writers who have other favorite authors and mentors so we can teach them what we know and learn techniques from them as well.

- **Benji and Annie:** Annie and I don't love memoir (sorry, Mrs. Murray!), so we would love other club members who like the genre better. Benji feels he is bad at editing his work, and Annie feels that she takes too long to draft. We would like help with that. But we both can come up with ideas for writing because we know that no matter what, you need to pick topics you know all about and love. We could help other writers with that.

Patty and Mrs. Murray were really blown away by the students' comments and knew that all the identity work in the launch unit was already paying off. So, they examined each partnership's index cards (yes, old-school index cards because they are much easier to manipulate) and put together clubs. They had to do a lot of shuffling, and even considered breaking up a partnership or two, but in the end decided against it. They wanted to honor the burgeoning writing relationships and not tinker with the partnerships just now, although that could be an option later in the year.

The next day's minilesson consisted of revealing the newly established clubs (at the beginning of the lesson) and demonstrating a strategy for generating ideas. This workshop day included the typical workshop writing time and then incorporated club time following the writing time. As was typical, the writing time ended with a wrap-up.

The first part of the minilesson actually started with students at their desks, ready with writing tools in hand. Patty then called students over, by club, and had a folder with three index cards in it: the original two composed by each partnership listing what they could share and what

Figure 3.6
Teacher Note to Process
Clubs with Rationale

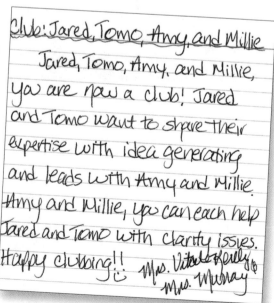

they would want from a club and a third from us. On this third index card, she told each club why she and Mrs. Murray had put them together. Those cards contained explanations such as:

- Jared, Tomo, Amy, and Ron, you are now a club. Jared and Tomo want to share their expertise with idea generating and leads with Amy and Ron. Amy and Ron, you can each help Jared and Tomo with clarity issues.

- Naomi, Rishon, Jeremy, and Raoul, you are now a club. Jeremy and Raoul, Naomi and Rishon are looking for more mentors, so share some of your favorite texts from Knucklehead. Naomi and Rishon, although you love your Sandra Cisneros, and I am sure you will share your love of her writing and her writing techniques, we think you can also offer strategies for notebook writing and ways you keep your stamina going.

The students were so excited by our comments, and even though it took time to compose those club identity cards, Patty and Mrs. Murray felt it was time well spent. In launching clubs in middle schools, where a teacher will have more than one section of students, we have seen teachers work in Google Classroom, so they can more easily manage the partner information and responses to students. We have also seen instances where the teacher orally shares reasons for putting students in certain clubs. This way, the information is communicated but not necessarily recorded for each club.

When clubs met that day during club time, they attended to a few "housekeeping items" regarding the club:

1. They named their club.

2. They found a home base meeting spot for their club.

3. They gathered any materials they would need. We had already provided each club with a folder and a bin, and each club added materials that were pertinent. For example, Amy introduced her club to her revision strips (lined, vertical sticky notes that she used to add and subtract for clarity), and Raoul made copies of his favorite vignettes for all of the members of his club to use as they moved through the unit.

Part Two: Lessons

Clubs were now under way. What happens next is that the unit continues, as usual, with the additional layer of process clubs. The teachers wanted to implement the memoir unit as expected, because it was a required unit in the fifth-grade curriculum calendar. They considered not only what layering this club experience would provide but also times for both the clubbing and the learning about process to happen. They decided on the following teaching points and learning opportunities.

A memoir unit is the ideal time to build identity, especially in grades five through eight. The unit can serve as an opportunity for a writer's coming of age journey, where the writer learns about this narrative genre as well as about themselves. Memoir also provides the opportunity to write to discover. Often, memoirists (even ones who are ten or twelve or fourteen) know what story they want to tell, but they don't quite know what the story is revealing about themselves. They write to discover that.

The teachers started by considering which prewriting (rehearsal) lessons to implement in the unit. One goal for the unit was that students could generate a variety of writing ideas, and another was that students would tell a story from their life that connects to their whole lives. Therefore, they decided to layer in two process minilessons:

1. An idea-generating minilesson on using the four windows of observation, memory, wonderings, and imagination to generate writing ideas.

2. An identity minilesson using micro-writing. Students think about who they are as a writer and write six-word memoirs to describe themselves. They can then do this same activity with memoir ideas.

It was during these two days that clubs would meet to share ideas and expertise and provide each other with feedback.

During the "writing" stage of the process, teachers decided that drafting would consist of each writer working independently on their draft and then having time to collaborate on craft work with their club. Students were exposed to a variety of memoir mentor texts during the first few days of the unit, and during the writing stage, they leaned on those texts alongside their club. Therefore, teachers planned for the following:

1. A minilesson on using a mentor text as a tool for generating writing. On that day during club time, students chose a club favorite and studied the text intently and collaboratively with each other.

2. Two club meetings within three days (purposely clustered together rather than spread across the week) so students could study mentors and try craft techniques, as well as write to discover their big ideas.

The last stage of the writing process is rewriting, which usually includes revising and editing. We believe that this stage of the unit and of the writing process is a prime opportunity to collaborate and share. Many writers love to share their writing, but here, we want to harness the power of feedback. Therefore, the teachers considered the following learning opportunities, drawing not only on the minilesson but on the midworkshop learning and the wrap-up:

- **Make Someone Famous.** As we confer with individuals and small groups during workshop, we always notice students doing great things. We believe it's important teaching to bring these acts of greatness to the attention of the other students, and a midworkshop teaching point is a prime opportunity to do so. Mrs. Murray looked for opportunities to make students famous and then asked each club to discuss what they had learned from that writer during their next club meeting. Few things are as motivating to students as seeing the work of their peers.

- **Club Share.** We often ask students to share the work they did that day with their long-term partner after we close things out. Here, Patty expanded this to the work of the club. The point of this activity was at first to provide clubs with an authentic audience. Mrs. Murray would wrap up the day by reiterating the teaching point, then ask students to share their writing with their club.

- **Quaker Share.** Sometimes we want to provide all our students with the opportunity to share with the whole group, rather than just their partner. When this is the case, we do a Quaker share.

A Quaker share is a structure used in Quaker meetings and is often called a "reading/sharing into the circle." In an effort to make these shares as brief as possible, we ask students to choose one specific thing to share with the group. We might ask students to share their favorite line from their current piece or their best sticky note. Process club Quaker shares envelop students in the beauty and power of language.

- **Sitting in the Chair Feedback Session.** Although we typically want all students to share their writing in some capacity, we occasionally opt for them to participate in a share session by providing feedback to one writer. Structured as a spin-off of the traditional author's chair (Graves and Hansen 1983), one writer sits in front of her community, asks for feedback in some capacity, and listens as writers provide her with possible ways she can revise her writing. The share ends with each writer (not just the writer sitting in the chair) committing to try one suggestion presented. Named "sitting in the chair" by one of Patty's former classes, this method of sharing is great for building a community of writers who support each other across the writing process. After a whole-class model of "sitting in the chair," clubs adopted this structure to provide each other with feedback.

Part Three: Clubbing Through Process Clubs

The previous section outlined ideas for what is taught and practiced in process clubs. In this section, we show you what it looks like when a unit with a complement club (such as process writing clubs) unfolds. Writing time always follows a predictable and student-oriented structure, and on club days, club time is layered in. A sample unit follows, showing one way a typical unit of study—in this case, a narrative unit in memoir, combined with a process club component—could unfold in a fifth-grade class. Please keep in mind that if there is nothing in the box for club time, there is no meeting during writing. If it states writing time in the box, students are writing as usual in workshop.

Figure 3.7
Sample Memoir Unit with Process Complement Clubs

Grade: 5 Unit: Memoir		Timeframe: Four Weeks		
	Day 1:	**Day 2:**	**Day 3:**	**Day 4:**	**Day 5:**

	Day 1:	**Day 2:**	**Day 3:**	**Day 4:**	**Day 5:**
Minilesson	Reading like a writer to explore memoir as a genre.	Universal truths in memoir writing.	Who are you as a writer? Six-word memoirs as people and with possible memoir ideas	Writing to discover: finding the big idea in the typical day	Idea generating using the four windows with an intro to clubs at the beginning of the lesson
Writing and Conferring	Writing time	Writing time	Writing time	Writing time	Writing time
Club Meeting					Initial club meeting
Wrap-Up	Notice, Name, and Note chart	Notice, Name, and Note chart; partner share	Quaker share	The big reveal of clubs; partner reflections	Make someone famous: idea generating that worked

	Day 6:	**Day 7:**	**Day 8:**	**Day 9:**	**Day 10:**
Minilesson	Using a mentor text to generate your own ideas	Five-minute review of Notice, Name, Note protocol	Structuring a memoir piece	Considering audience	Drafting strategy
Club Meeting	Study a favorite mentor text; list three ways this can inspire your own writing	Study mentor texts; notice and name craft techniques to try			

Figure 3.7 (continued)
Sample Memoir Unit with Process Complement Clubs

	Day 6 (cont'd):	Day 7 (cont'd):	Day 8 (cont'd):	Day 9 (cont'd):	Day 10 (cont'd):
Writing and Conferring	Writing time	Writing time	Writing time and midworkshop: make someone famous—idea generating using a mentor author as inspiration	Writing time	Writing time
Wrap-Up	Idea share: what one writes about, more might write about	Adding to our memoir chart	Whole-class Quaker share of powerful line	Wrap-up/club time: provide feedback on entries written using the inspiration and techniques learned	Clubs sit together and have a quick reflection convo; share draft reflections

	Day 11:	Day 12:	Day 13:	Day 14:	Day 15:
Minilesson	Finding the heart of your story	Adding inside story: what you thought, saw, and felt	Reflective endings in memoir texts	Drafting another memoir piece	Changing point of view: an invitation to try third-person narrative writing
Writing and Conferring	Writing time	Writing time	Writing time	Writing time	Writing time
Club Meeting			Sitting in the chair protocol		Sitting in the chair protocol
Wrap-Up	Sitting in the chair protocol, whole group	Sharing examples of "internal thinking"	Does your ending reflect your truth?	Drafting reflections	Club reflections chart

	Day 16:	Day 17:	Day 18:	Day 19:	Day 20:
Minilesson	Circular structure in memoir texts	Revision: What do we leave in? What do we take out?	Editing for clarity	Publishing toward your audience	Writing celebration and club reflection
Writing and Conferring	Writing time	Writing time	Writing time	Writing time	
Club Meeting	Sitting in the chair protocol	*No official club time. Clubs may choose to meet.*	*No official club time. Clubs may choose to meet.*	*No official club time. Clubs may choose to meet.*	
Wrap-Up	Three-minute quick share with each club sharing what is working well	Club feedback on revisions	Checking up on our checklist	Preparing for celebration	

STUDENT SAMPLE

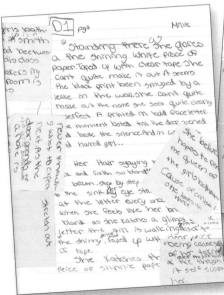

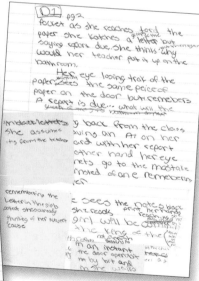

Figure 3.8
One Student Responds To
Feedback from Her Club

Figure 3.8
One Student Responds To
Feedback from Her Club

The Girls Bathroom

The girls bathroom is in Smith school between Mrs. Doyle's class and a bunch of crunched in, small, tan lockers. Her classroom is across from Mrs. Doyle's class room.

Never knowing what to expect next, as the door opens slowly, a note is waiting on the door!

As she, the red-haired girl, glares at the shinning piece of paper taped up, there's a name she can't make out on the front of the cover. As her eyes roll down the front of the paper the door opens breaking the silence. In walks a blond haired girl. . .

Her hair swaying back and forth as the light reflected on her, the blond-haired girl made her way to the sink. As she pushes the door open, with her hair still wet, her hair is still shimmering. Then the red-haired girl's eye catches a glimpse of the first four words,
   The report is due..

With her mind confused, she's thinking, *why would the teacher hang that up in the girls bathroom?"* As she takes four slow steps backward she sees that same piece of paper is still on the door. Looking at the paper with relief she remembers a report is due. . .

As she once again walks in the bathroom door days later, with a report card in one hand and the report in the other, her eye went straight to a mistake, a lower case I instead of a Capital I. Then remembering the letter on the door, her hands draw closer and closer as she picks up the lid. With fear she reads,

A NEW GIRL IS COMING. SHE IS THE QUEEN OF THE GIRLS BATHROOM!

She's hoping it's a joke. A jingle could be heard as the door then opens and a blue eyed girl walks in...

                                       Millie

LIFE AFTER PROCESS CLUBS

Now that a complement club has been added to a typical unit, teachers have endless possibilities for what they might do next, including:

- Choose to examine your year and find places where other complement clubs would enhance a unit of study. Possibilities include tucking a craft or social justice club into any unit of study. Although you've just implemented a process club in your memoir (or any other genre unit), you may actually add another process club to a different unit of study. Why? Because the habits, routines, and processes that a writer uses are both varied and essential to their growth and development as a writer. Therefore, other process skills not heavily addressed in this unit would enhance a genre experience and cultivate collaboration and process skills of any writer. Additionally, a writer's process will vary when they work on different kinds of writing.

- Choose to implement a club unit! A stand-alone club unit will create variety to the school year and allow students to make choices and decisions as writers that they often don't get to experience in more typical genre units. Our favorites are genre clubs, conventions clubs, and author clubs. Author clubs provide students with an opportunity to study both the "office work" (Ray 1999) and craft of a favorite author with like-minded students. Students who have been disengaged or avoiding writing in the past may just become more inspired and engaged via a club experience.

Chapter 4

Craft Clubs: Studying Mentor Texts Together

ecently, Lisa was asked to write a graduation letter for a close friend's high school senior. She immediately agreed—she had known the child for most of her life and adored her. However, Lisa didn't know what a graduation letter was or what it entailed. After doing some digging, she discovered it is a letter to the graduate recounting memories of them growing up and also offers advice about anything from college to life and everything in between. The letters are requested from friends and family, bundled up, and gifted to the graduate on the morning of their senior breakfast where many are read aloud (no pressure there). Never having written such a letter before, Lisa did what all writers do: she sought out some mentor texts. An email and a few text messages later, she had collected quite a few samples.

Before putting pen to paper, Lisa read. In her initial readings of the letters, she paid close attention to the required elements, trying to determine the general expectations of this new genre. Once she understood the general requirements, she began writing. Throughout her drafting and revising, she returned repeatedly to several of her favorite letters. She admired the overall essay structure of one letter and mimicked it in her own. Humorous and touching anecdotes were peppered throughout another, creating an amusing but heartfelt tone that she tried to emulate. She adored the closing advice in one and ended her letter in a similar manner.

Lisa mailed the letter and forgot about it until a couple of months later when she received a text from the now graduated senior who thanked her for her kind words, told her the letter was one of her favorites, and said she would treasure it forever. Lisa could have written the letter without studying the mentor texts, but would it have had the same impact? We think not. Like all writers, studying mentor texts and emulating craft moves from other authors makes your writing better and also makes you a better writer. This is our goal for craft clubs: for students to study the work of other authors, emulate their craft moves, and, in the end, become better writers. Let's begin.

PREPARING FOR CRAFT CLUBS

Before jumping into craft complement clubs, we have to do a few things to ensure this club runs smoothly.

Gathering Materials

Craft clubs, like most clubs, don't require you to gather a lot of additional materials. As students are clubbing through a unit, they will be using materials they typically use during writing time such as writer's notebooks, anchor charts, checklists, and a writing center. In addition to these items, craft clubs will require you to have a few mentor texts for each club to study. We suggest four to six different titles per club to keep things manageable for both the teacher and the students. For example, in a third-grade classroom where we were incorporating craft clubs into a nonfiction chapter book unit, we had twenty-four students. Therefore, we made six clubs with four students, knowing we would need six copies of each nonfiction mentor text for club work.

Choosing Mentor Texts for Craft Clubs

Choosing mentor texts for craft clubs can seem daunting. We live in a time when thousands of beautiful children's books are published each year. It is tempting to load kids down with all of the beautiful books we love, but we have found that less is more. We choose a few of our favorite mentor texts, ones we know well, for craft clubs. When deciding on mentor texts, we also keep in mind the level of our students. For example, we love Sandra Cisneros, and her texts can teach students so much about what it means to write well. However, her level of writing is beyond most students' ability until about fifth grade. When choosing mentor texts for clubs, we try to choose books we know well and believe offer techniques kids are ready to tackle. In Figure 4.1, we provide a list of some of our favorite mentor texts that we use across grade levels and genres to support craft clubs.

Figure 4.1
Some of Our Favorite Mentor Texts for Craft Clubs

Pecan Pie Baby by Jacqueline Woodson

Crow Call by Lois Lowry

Jabari Jumps by Gaia Cornwell

Last Stop On Market Street by Matt de la Peña

A Pig Parade Is a Terrible Idea by Michael Ian Black

My Brother Dan's Delicious by Steven L. Layne

Dear Basketball (A letter in The Player's Tribune) by Kobe Bryant

I Am Loved by Nikki Giovanni

Grandfather's Journey by Allen Say

The Big Box by Toni Morrison

The House on Mango Street by Sandra Cisneros

14 Cows for America by Carmen Agra Deedy

The Dream Keeper and Other Poems by Langston Hughes

Actual Size by Steve Jenkins

Spiders by Seymour Simon

Hurricanes by Gail Gibbons

Deadliest Animals by Melissa Stewart

I'm New Here by Anne Sibley O'Brien

Family Pictures by Carmen Lomas Garza

Peter's Chair by Ezra Jack Keats

The Other Side by Jacqueline Woodson (OR *Each Kindness* by Jacqueline Woodson)

A Sweet Smell of Roses by Angela Johnson

Water Music by Jane Yolen

Envisioning How the Work Will Go

In Chapter 2, we provide options for how writing clubs can fit into the existing fabric of writing time. Complement clubs are part of the writing workshop, borrowing time from the independent practice and share. In some clubs, students meet as a whole group for a minilesson, go off and write independently, pause their independent writing to meet with their club for a few minutes, and then the class wraps up. In craft clubs, we have found it more effective to have students meet in their clubs right after the minilesson and before they begin writing. We structure craft clubs

this way so students can immediately implement what they learned with their group when they begin writing that day. We also allow more time in the wrap-up for students to get feedback on their writing from their club.

When Will Craft Clubs Happen?

Many complement clubs do not meet every week during a unit. Instead, teachers choose the work they want to do with students and decide when to add clubs based on what students need. For example, in process clubs, teachers might want to support students as they rehearse and play in their notebooks, so they will opt to add writing clubs into that week's work as extra support for a couple of days. We implement craft clubs when students are focusing more on crafting their writing. This shift in focus generally happens when students are drafting and revising.

Teaching Points to Consider

If you input "qualities" or "traits" of writing into a search engine, a plethora of results show up (we found 158,000,000 when we entered it into Google). Obviously, many people have a lot to say about what constitutes good writing. As we consider all the things we know about good writing, and all the things we could teach students about crafting writing, we realize we must teach a few key qualities. Among these qualities is a hierarchy—not all traits are created equal. Some are more important because of the impact they have on writing. Figure 4.2 on page 72 shows how we view the traits of writing with a brief definition of each. We have listed the qualities from the most important to the least (Eickholdt 2015). We also provide guiding questions to help students make theories about the writing work. This is inquiry work at its best. A key to this work is that students know they will not only notice craft elements but also emulate them in their own writing.

CLUB TIME

In complement craft clubs students read the same text many times. These close readings help students gain insight and appreciation for the author's craft.

Part One: Forming and Launching Clubs

Though craft clubs won't commence until students are drafting, we like to determine how we're grouping students at the start of the unit. Therefore, this club begins with students assessing themselves as writers.

Self-Assessment

As with any club, we avoid placing students in groups without their input. In craft clubs, we ask students to provide us with feedback about their writing through self-assessment. We have a couple of ways we might ask students to conduct this self-assessment. If our upcoming genre study is similar to a genre we've previously studied—perhaps we are moving from writing personal narratives to writing realistic fiction—we provide students with their last published piece to assess. Using sticky notes, students

Figure 4.2
Hierarchy of Writing Qualities

Writing Qualities	Definition
Focus	Writing should have a focus on a moment, idea, or message. Focus is the most important quality because it affects all the others. Focus brings clarity to a piece. • What is the focus of this piece? Is it about a moment, event, or idea? • How does the author convey their focus? • How can you emulate these moves?
Structure	Structure refers to how the piece is organized or put together. A text should include elements of the genre, including various text structures. The writer should group ideas in meaningful ways with important parts or ideas emphasized and unimportant parts or ideas excluded or deemphasized. What are the key elements of this kind of writing? • What kinds of text structures does the author use? • Did the author emphasize important parts or ideas? • How does the writer hook you with their lead? • How do they wrap things up with their ending? • How can you emulate these moves?
Elaboration	Elaborating is often described as adding more details or telling more. Writers elaborate by showing, not telling, or with explanation and example. Much of what we teach kids about writing well has to do with elaboration. • How did the writer elaborate the most important parts? • How do you think the writer chose parts to elaborate? • How did the writer show, not tell? • How can you emulate these moves?
Word Choice	Word choice paints a picture for the reader or makes things clearer. It helps the reader envision people, places, and things and put themself in the story. • Did the writer use juicy or expert words? • Did the writer use five-sense language? • Did the writer write with specificity? • How can you emulate these moves?

mark the places they feel are strong and the places they think need work. If the unit we are embarking on isn't one we've studied with our kids, we ask students to write an initial on-demand piece (Calkins, Hohne, and Robb 2013). Afterward, we ask them to self-assess, comparing their writing to the exemplar texts we've studied. In both cases, after students have had time to reflect on their writing, we ask them to jot down their answers to the following questions on index cards and discuss them with their writing partners:

1. What do you think you can most offer a craft club?

2. What support do you want from a craft club?

After students have discussed their responses with their partners, we gather their index cards so we can use them to create clubs. As we form clubs, we are looking for a balance of strengths and goals. For example, we often group a student who states that endings are their strength with a student who believes endings are an area of need for them, so they can support one another during the unit.

Launching Craft Clubs

We find it helpful to announce the newly formed craft clubs at the end of workshop a day or two before they will begin. After we remind students that we are adding clubs to our current writing unit and their cheers and high-fives have subsided, we call students up by club, remind them of their self-assessments, and explain the reasons we grouped them based on their feedback. After we reveal students' clubs, we provide time for them to meet and establish club basics such as finding a place in the room to meet and giving their group a name. The next day, we use our minilesson time to introduce students to the mentor texts they will be studying and give them a time to peruse the texts before they write. In a third-grade nonfiction study, we chose the following nonfiction books for our craft clubs:

Snakes! by Melissa Stewart

Hurricanes by Gail Gibbons

What Do You Do with a Tail Like This? by Steve Jenkins

Tadpole to Frog by Shira Evans

In addition to these books, we also added to each tub a couple of copies of *Zoobooks*, which were readily available from the school's bookroom. We didn't have multiple copies of the same title, but we weren't concerned. Each magazine possessed many of the important informational writing qualities we would be teaching in the study, so we felt confident with this additional choice.

What If Craft Clubs Are Inside a Remote or Hybrid Unit?

Writing clubs have become a powerful and effective way to continue student collaborations in the age of hybrid and remote teaching. Craft clubs are easy to implement, if you are teaching in a hybrid, HyFlex, or remote setting.

When teaching in one of the above-mentioned alternate settings, we launch the craft club online. We ask students to go through the same self-assessment process and collect their responses in the form of a digital document rather than an index card. After we announce the student clubs, including the rationale as to why we placed students in certain clubs, we put the clubs into breakout rooms so they can meet, discuss club protocols, and have an opportunity to check in with their new community of collaborators.

The next day, just as in the in-person model, we use our minilesson time to introduce students to the mentor texts they will be studying and give them a time to peruse the texts before they write. We choose texts that are available digitally in the form of ebooks and add the magazine/article component as well. One easy way to organize the materials is to create a digital bin with the text options, as well as links to other pertinent club docs (planners, craft charts, and Google or Kami docs of notes or student samples) for each club. Figure 4.3 shows some possible ebook platforms that teachers and students can use for digital craft clubs.

Figure 4.3
Digital Reading Options

Platform	Pros	Subscription
Epic	Epic has a diverse collection of original books and trade books that are appealing to kids and filled with craft from which students can learn.	Epic is a subscription platform; however, Epic was free to students at various times during 2020.
TumbleBooks	TumbleBooks is a reasonably priced collection of ebooks containing titles from some of our most-beloved authors.	Well-priced subscription fee.
myON	MyON is a platform of more than 6,000 titles from a diverse array of quality publishers.	Subscription fee.
Public library subscriptions	Local public libraries contain subscriptions to various free ereading platforms. Possibilities include: Libby (libbyapp.com), Hoopla (hoopladigital.com), and even BookFlix and TrueFlix by Scholastic (emea.scholastic.com).	Free.

Part Two: Lessons

When envisioning the work students will do in craft clubs within any unit, we must begin by assessing students and considering what they need most to improve their writing. Then, we design our craft clubs to support and extend these concepts. We recommend assessing your group's writing before any new unit of study to help you determine your teaching focus. As we gather students' writing and self-assessments in search of ways to group them into clubs, we are also looking at the group as a whole and assessing their instructional needs. As we read through their writing, we keep in mind the many aspects of writing and the hierarchy of the various qualities. To guide our assessment, we ask similar questions to the ones we provide students with when they study the craft of writing in their club. Figure 4.4 shows an example of some of the questions we consider as we study the groups' work.

Figure 4.4
Guiding Assessment Questions

Focus
• Did the writer focus their piece? Is it about a moment, event, or idea?
• Does the author convey a message?

Structure
• Did the writer include the key elements of this kind of writing?
• Is their structure or structures effective?
• Did they exclude unimportant or extraneous parts and ideas and emphasize important ones?
• Did the writer craft an interesting lead?
• Did they craft an ending that wrapped things up?

Elaboration
• What elaboration techniques did the writer use?
• Did the writer elaborate the important parts?
• Did the writer show, not tell?

Word Choice
• Did the writer use juicy or expert words?
• Did the writer use five-sense language?
• Did the writer write with specificity?

When we assessed our third-grade students' writing, we noticed they were doing a good job with focus, staying on topic throughout their pieces, but they needed additional help with structure and elaboration. Therefore, when we planned the unit with the classroom teacher, we emphasized both of these elements. Based on students' feedback and our whole-group assessment, we made some decisions regarding how the unit would unfold.

Because many students stated in their self-assessments that they wanted assistance with leads and endings, we decided to provide lessons and club time for the study of each concept. Though we often teach lead techniques during revision, we can also teach them when students begin drafting, which was when the classroom teacher planned to teach them in this unit. However, the teacher would teach endings as a revision strategy near the conclusion of the study.

If there is a secret to writing, we believe it is elaboration. Because we think elaboration is one of the most important things students can learn in any genre, we knew we would spend lots of time teaching students these strategies. In narrative writing, we often tell students to show, not tell. In nonnarrative writing, we teach students to tell and show (Calkins and Gillette 2006). Therefore, we knew that we would spend a good deal of lesson and club time demonstrating our favorite informational elaboration strategies, such as using an anecdote, quotes, or numbers to add details. We also knew we would provide students with plenty of time to discover other techniques from their mentor texts.

In informational writing, word choice is important. Students must define vocabulary words in various ways throughout a text to support the reader. Students tend to enjoy learning vocabulary techniques, and these are easy to add into a text at any point in the process, so we decided we would teach them as students revised their pieces.

Knowing what to teach and when to teach it is important, but we must also consider how we instruct. In this unit, we knew we would take advantage of the inquiry nature of clubs. To this end, in many of our minilessons, we teach one writing technique and then send students off to read and discover more with their clubs before they move to independent writing, where they try out all they have learned. Because we see great value in using student writing as a mentor text, we are always sure to leave lots of time to highlight club work and students' discoveries by making clubs famous during the minilesson or at the end-of-day wrap-up.

Part Three: Clubbing Through Craft Clubs

An example of how this informational unit with craft clubs unfolded in one third-grade classroom follows. Please keep in mind that if the club meeting box is empty, there is no meeting during writing. If the box states writing time, students are writing as usual in workshop.

Figure 4.5
Sample Informational Unit with Craft Complement Clubs

Grade: _3_   Unit: _Nonfiction Chapter Books_   Timeframe: _Four Weeks_

	Day 1:	Day 2:	Day 3:	Day 4:	Day 5:
Minilesson	Reading like a writer to explore nonfiction chapter books as a genre	Reading like a writer to explore nonfiction chapter books as a genre	Reading like a writer to explore nonfiction chapter books as a genre	No minilesson. On-demand informational writing assessment	Using what we know about good writing to assess our own
Writing and Conferring	Studying mentor texts using notice, name, and note	Studying mentor texts using notice, name, and note	Studying mentor texts using notice, name, and note	Writing assessment	Self-assess your informational writing
Club Meeting					
Wrap-Up	Beginning an anchor chart listing key elements from the genre	Adding to the anchor chart from day 1	Adding to the anchor chart from day 1	No wrap-up due to assessment	Reflection and discussion of self-assessment

	Day 6:	Day 7:	Day 8:	Day 9:	Day 10:
Minilesson	Idea generation: What are you an expert on? What can you teach others about?	Mentor texts revealed	Informational leads: starting with an interesting fact	Make a club famous for discovering a lead technique	Informational text structures: main idea with supporting details
Club Meeting		Study mentor texts	Study leads in mentor text	Study leads in mentor text	
Writing and Conferring	Exploring expert topics	Using quick writes to determine the best topic	Writing time	Writing time	Writing time

	Day 6 (cont'd):	Day 7 (cont'd):	Day 8 (cont'd):	Day 9 (cont'd):	Day 10 (cont'd):
Wrap-Up	Clubs revealed	Sharing our topics	Group share of interesting leads	Clubs share and get feedback on leads	Share student samples of main idea structure

	Day 11:	Day 12:	Day 13:	Day 14:	Day 15:
Minilesson	Make a club or student famous for discovering a text structure	Nonfiction elaboration strategy: adding details with partner facts	Nonfiction elaboration strategy: adding details by using quotes	Make a club or student famous for discovering an elaboration technique	Nonfiction elaboration strategy: adding details with numbers
Club Meeting			Study elaboration techniques		Study elaboration techniques
Writing and Conferring	Writing time	Writing time	Writing time	Writing time	Writing time
Wrap-Up	Museum share of text structures (students label with sticky notes in preparation)	Group adds to a class elaboration chart	Clubs share and get feedback on elaboration techniques	Clubs share and get feedback on elaboration techniques	Group adds to a class elaboration chart

	Day 16:	Day 17:	Day 18:	Day 19:	Day 20:
Minilesson	Vocabulary strategies	Make several groups famous for vocabulary strategies	Revising endings: end with a call to action	Editing and getting writing ready for publishing	Writing celebration and club reflection
Club Meeting	Study vocabulary strategies		Study endings	*No official club time. Clubs may choose to meet.	

Figure 4.5 (continued)
Sample Informational Unit with Craft Complement Clubs

		Day 16 (cont'd):	Day 17 (cont'd):	Day 18 (cont'd):	Day 19 (cont'd):	Day 20 (cont'd):
Writing and Conferring		Writing time: create a glossary to define vocabulary words	Writing time	Writing time	Writing time	Writing celebration and club reflection
Wrap-Up		Sharing glossaries	Sharing vocabulary strategies	Clubs share and get feedback on endings	Preparing for celebration	

STUDENT SAMPLES

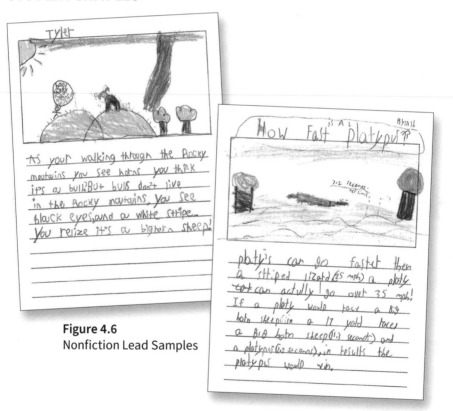

Figure 4.6
Nonfiction Lead Samples

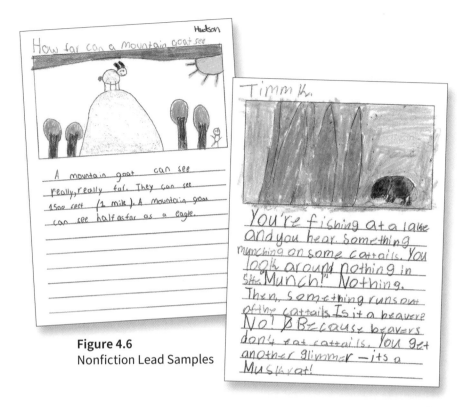

Figure 4.6
Nonfiction Lead Samples

LIFE AFTER CRAFT CLUBS

When craft clubs commence, we notice students have gained a new appreciation and interest in the authors of our club books. During the study or afterward, students begin seeking out other books by our mentor authors. We are happy to assist them in their search. We believe exposing students to new authors and books is one of the most important jobs of any literacy teacher. Some students want to know more about their favorite writer, and, again, we are happy to help. We show students authors' websites, help them keep up with their favorite writer's latest publishing, and show the students how to follow them on social media. This new love for authors is a great thing because it moves students to become more avid readers and writers. Another reason we value all this author love is that we know we will build on it with a stand-alone author club later in the year.

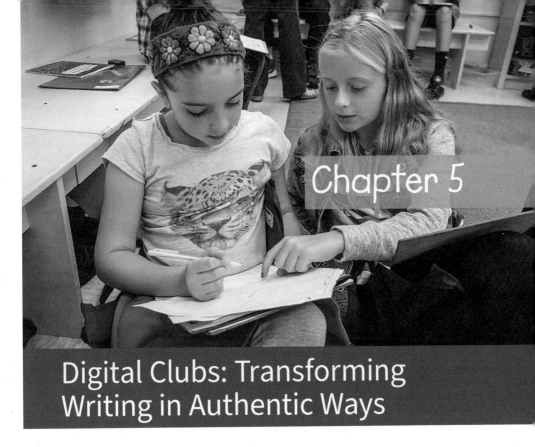

Chapter 5

Digital Clubs: Transforming Writing in Authentic Ways

A few years ago, Lisa was working in a fourth-grade classroom. About a month was left in the school year—the time the teacher, Leslie, and Lisa often used to try out something new. They loved to experiment with instructional practices at the end of the year because it helped keep everyone excited about learning. It also allowed them to work out any bugs before adding the new concept to their instruction the next year. Leslie and Lisa also knew they needed to plan something for their school's annual step-up day. Step-up day was the day incoming students were invited to step up to their new grade level to meet their teachers and get a preview of some of the exciting things they would be doing the next year. Leslie was searching for a way to make this step-up day more meaningful. She usually spent time showing the incoming students her class library and talking up some of her favorite books. She wondered what would happen if she invited her current students to help this year. She discussed it with Lisa and came up with a plan. They could create digital book trailers for their favorite books and attach QR codes to them. Then on step-up day, the incoming students could scan the codes and view the book trailers. When she presented the idea to her fourth-grade students, they were thrilled! They loved the idea of creating book trailers for their younger peers and siblings. They also loved that these trailers would remain linked to Leslie's books for years to come.

Leslie and Lisa began the unit by reviewing the elements of a book review, something students had written earlier in the year. Then, they showed them lots of book trailers so they had an idea of what they'd be creating. Students partnered up based on their book choice and began storyboarding their plans for their trailer as we booked time in the computer lab. After several weeks, the trailers were complete and ready for viewing. On step-up day, the fourth graders asked to stay in class part of the time, so they could present their book trailers to the younger students. Excitement filled the air as kids sat side-by-side viewing the trailers and talking about books. Watching students share their book trailers with their younger peers and siblings was wonderful. As we reflect on our teaching, the book trailer unit is one we remember fondly. This digital project brought a renewed sense of energy and purpose for everyone. Engaging work such as the kind kids did in this book trailer project is our goal when adding digital clubs as a complement to any unit of study. Let's see how we can accomplish it.

PREPARING FOR DIGITAL CLUBS

Like many of you, we are not digital natives. Growing up, we had no technology standards, and the only technology in our classrooms was a chalkboard (yes, a real chalkboard, not a whiteboard, and certainly not an interactive whiteboard). Times have changed over the last thirty years, and now in our schools, as in our society, it seems technology is everywhere. Even very young students have phones that provide them with access to the world. Adding technology to teaching is something we know all educators are required to do to meet new technology standards—and *should* do to build on kids' natural interest in all things digital. However, integrating technology into teaching is fraught with the risk that it will be used in ineffective or inauthentic ways. In other words, we don't want to *do* technology for technology's sake.

Sometimes we see technology being used as a digital version of skill-and-drill worksheets—something we definitely try to avoid. We also want to be sure that when we add technology to our instruction, it doesn't foster what Donalyn Miller once called a "language arts and crafts" curriculum (https://bookwhisperer.com/2014/09/07/), such as requiring students to create the digital equivalent of a diorama after completing a book. Instead, we should use technology to transform writing in genuine ways, such as asking students to create digital book trailers for rising peers. We have seen the advantages of adding digital clubs to units of study: increased engagement, authentic collaboration, and a new level of interest in the work due to a wider audience. So, as we consider adding digital clubs to a unit of study, we keep in mind what not to do, which helps us consider what to do.

When envisioning how we will use digital clubs to complement a current unit of study, we have found it helpful to consider the SAMR model. SAMR, which stands for substitution, augmentation, modification, and redefinition, was created by Dr. Reuben Puentedura and supports teachers as they integrate technology into their classroom (http://www.hippasus.com/rrpweblog/archives/2014/12/11/SAMRandTPCK_HandsOnApproachClassroomPractice.pdf). Many educators who use the model aim to "work above the line"—the line being the division between the bottom two elements—substitution and augmentation, which are considered enhancements—and the top two elements—modification and redefinition, which are considered transformative practices.

In *Amplify* (Muhtaris and Ziemke 2015), the authors define the difference in the top levels of the model: "At this level (modification), technology becomes transformative and allows us to redesign the task. . . . Lastly comes redefinition, where teachers can create entirely new tasks never thought possible" (page xiv). Therefore, when adding digital clubs to any unit of study, we try to work above the line and integrate technology in ways that modify and transform students' writing. To do so, we have found it helpful to consider how to marry technology to our writing workshop in authentic ways and for a broader audience. We begin by considering our unit of study and then choose ways that naturally extend our kids' writing. For example, we recently added digital clubs to a fourth-grade poetry unit. After spending a couple of weeks studying and writing poetry, we encouraged students to create digital poems to add to a class book, which was later shared with parents during our annual poetry café. Figure 5.1 shows some of the ways digital clubs could complement various units of study and expand students' audience.

Figure 5.1
Digital Clubs as a Complement to Various Units of Study

Unit of Study	Digital Complement	Audience
Poetry	Digital poetry	Share poetry with parents and peers at annual poetry café.
Argument Essays	Public service announcement	Share the public service announcement on the Web via the school's blog, Twitter, or SchoolTube account.
Procedural Texts	Video tutorial	Create a video showing how to perform a task for peers.
Fiction	Digital storybook	Create a digital storybook for younger students or book buddies.
Informational Text	A multitouch book (embedded links, video, and audio)	Create a multitouch book to share with peers from another classroom.
Book Reviews	Book trailers	Create a QR code and attach it to copies of the book to share the trailers with students coming to the grade level next year (a great end-of-year unit), or place it in the library for the whole school to enjoy.

Gathering Materials

In addition to the materials students use each day as they write, the primary materials you will need for digital clubs are access to a computer or device and a digital platform. The good news is that every child doesn't have to have their own device to implement this complement club. In most of the schools we work in, teachers do not have constant access to technology; instead, computer labs or laptop carts are available at the school, and teachers arrange to use them. We suggest reserving lab time or computer carts early on when planning your unit. Once the hardware is in place, we need to choose software.

Choosing a platform for digital clubs can be overwhelming. Thousands of applications and programs are created each year, and choosing the one that best fits your and your students' needs can make your head spin. We begin by deciding on the kind of writing we will use as a complement to our digital unit. Then we turn to the most reliable resource we know for help: fellow educators. We might make an appointment to see our school's technology support person and seek their guidance. We may email teacher friends who we consider techies and ask for their advice. Or we may tap into the power of the Web and use an Internet search engine to help us locate fellow educators who have done similar work with their students and examine the platform they've used. Once we've got a few choices in mind, we examine each one more closely. We peruse the site or app, look at samples, and read what other educators have to say about it. We are looking for platforms that have several key attributes: they are user friendly, they are readily available (perhaps already available at our school), and they are free or inexpensive. In Figure 5.2, we provide a list of some of our favorite platforms and the ways we might use them in digital writing clubs.

Figure 5.2
Some of Our Current Favorite Digital Platforms

Platform	Digital Format
Animoto	Digital poetry Book trailers
YouTube	How-to videos Public service announcements Video essays
WeVideo	Book trailers Digital poetry
Storybird	Stories Digital poetry
Comic Creator	Comics Fairy tales

Figure 5.2 (continued)
Some of Our Current Favorite Digital Platforms

Platform	Digital Format
Powtoon	Book trailers How-to videos
Book Creator	Multitouch informational books Stories

Envisioning How the Work Will Go

When envisioning how digital clubs will play out in any classroom, the first consideration is to determine how the digital work will augment the writing in the current unit. One way to add digital clubs is to encourage students to create something that directly extends the writing they are already doing in the unit. If we examine the digital poetry example we mentioned earlier in the chapter, we see this as a natural extension of the poetry unit. We implement clubs and encourage students to use all they've learned about writing poems to create digital versions. Though a digital poem requires different skills to create, it complements our poetry study because our students' current writing work helps them do the new work. For example, when teaching students about poetry, we teach them about the power of imagery and how poets paint pictures with their words. Students can easily take this idea of imagery into a digital poem and use real images to enhance their words.

When Will Digital Clubs Happen?

One key way digital clubs differ from other clubs is in the time we devote to them each day. In most complement clubs, we plan for groups to meet for ten or fifteen minutes a day during workshop. This is not feasible with digital clubs because students need time to create their project using the available technology. Therefore, once we implement digital clubs, we dedicate the whole day's writing time to digital work and add a club meeting. For us that means holding our writing workshop in the school's computer lab for the day.

Another way digital clubs differ from other clubs is in the timing. In most complement clubs, we examine the current writing unit, determine when students might need the most support, and launch the clubs during this time. Though digital clubs build on the writing students are currently doing in a unit, they do require kids to create something new. Therefore, we implement them when we think adding in this new writing will make the most sense—generally about midway through the unit. For example, when adding digital poetry clubs to a poetry unit of study, we generally launch and teach students lessons about writing poetry for a couple of weeks, then we pause for about one week to focus on digital work. This pause in the unit is important. We use this week to introduce students to the genre of digital poetry, the platform they will be using, form clubs, and allow students to create a few digital poems. After this weeklong pause, we weave digital clubs into our instruction a couple days a week, like we do with other complement clubs. The unit then continues in this way—students write poems traditionally a few days a week, then meet with their clubs to plan and compose digital poems on the other days.

If we are asking students to create a single digital piece, we still implement clubs about midway through the unit, and then we focus on that work every day for the rest of the study. For example, if students are in an argument essay unit, and we want them to create a public service announcement based on all they've learned from writing their essay, we will introduce digital clubs midway through the unit, but then we will ask students to focus on this digital aspect every day for the duration of the study.

Teaching Points to Consider

We believe that teachers need to do everything they ask of their students first, not only because it makes instruction more authentic but because it helps them know what to teach. Incorporating digital clubs into writing workshop is no exception; we must begin by doing the work ourselves. As you create the digital piece, take careful notes of what you did and how you did it. Later, you can go back to your notes and use them to plan minilessons for your clubs. Figure 5.3 on page 90 shows a table with Lisa's recent reflections on the work she did as she created a digital poem and her reflections on how this work can help her plan upcoming lessons.

Figure 5.3
Reflecting to Plan Lessons

Question	Reflection	How Does This Help Me Teach?
How did I choose something to create?	I chose a poem from my notebook.	To generate ideas, ask students to peruse their notebooks for poems they think would be good digitized.
How did I add imagery to my poem?	I chose pictures from the Web to add to my poem.	Demonstrate for students where to find copyright-free images to add to their poem.
How did I revise my poem?	I went back in and changed the line breaks so the words flowed with more rhythm.	Show students how breaking the lines up changes the way the poem is read.
How did I edit my poem for publication?	I played with the font size, color, and shape.	Show students how different font shapes, sizes, and colors can impact the mood of a poem.

CLUB TIME

Digital complement clubs add so much excitement to any writing unit. Students enjoy composing new pieces or seeing a traditional piece come to life in a whole new way.

Part One: Forming and Launching Digital Clubs

Digital clubs aren't launched until we've worked in the unit for at least two weeks. We wait to group kids into clubs until they've had time to preview what they will be creating and work a bit in the platform we've chosen.

Beginning at the Beginning: Self-Assessment

As with any club, we avoid placing students in groups without their input. In digital clubs, we create groupings based on students' feelings about both the digital content and tool. In exploring any new kind of writing, we believe students must read before they write. Therefore, we begin by immersing students in the digital format they will be creating for a day or so. Once students have a vision for their upcoming work, we introduce the platform and let them play with it. We recommend building in at least one day of free exploration. This play-before-you-work concept is similar to allowing students to explore math manipulatives before working with them. It helps kids get acquainted with the platform and allows them to discover how it works. After they've been immersed in the project and the platform, we ask them to assess how they feel about both. We have found rating scales to be effective for this self-assessment. Figure 5.4 shows an example of an emoji rating scale we recently used with kids who were going to use Powtoon to create book trailers.

Figure 5.4
Emoji Rating Scale

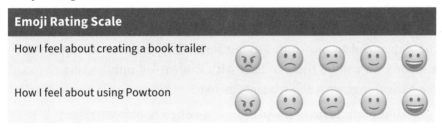

Launching Digital Clubs

After we collect students' rating scales, we examine them closely, trying to create clubs with a balance of expertise. We like to group students who feel very comfortable with the platform and less so with the content with students who feel the opposite way. This ensures we have a balance of strengths students can draw upon as they work in clubs.

Part Two: Lessons

The instruction in digital clubs tends to fall into one of three categories: lessons on how to use the platform, lessons that build on or extend key concepts we are teaching students about writing in that genre, and lessons where the digital writing leads the writing.

Lessons on Using the Platform

In digital clubs, we know we must include lessons on how to use the platform effectively. We begin by teaching students the fundamentals of using the platform, such as logging in, adding images and words, and

saving their work. Once we teach students a few basics, we step aside and encourage them to teach us. When it comes to using technology, we can't think of a better time to let our students lead the way. Therefore, at the end of workshop we often ask students to share things they've discovered about how to best use the platform and add these to an ongoing anchor chart of tips and tricks. We also plan for the unplanned in our unit: leaving some days' minilesson topics open, knowing we will fill them in later with student-led minilessons. Some of the basic things we teach students include:

- How to navigate to the platform (we often bookmark these)
- How to log on
- How to begin creating within the platform
- How to use the basic tools within the platform
- How to clear unwanted elements
- How and where to save ongoing work
- How to access ongoing work later

Extending Key Lessons

Because digital clubs are designed to build on students' writing work within a unit, we find it helpful to link these lessons whenever possible. Let's consider some of the key lessons we might teach our fourth graders in our poetry study. One of the big ideas we teach students in this unit is that poems are built on three pillars: emotion, imagery, and music (Portalupi and Fletcher 2004). We design many lessons around these three pillars. We teach students various craft moves to add imagery to poems, such as using similes and metaphors, personification, and onomatopoeia.

We teach them to add music or rhythm by using line breaks and white spaces, repetition, and alliteration. As students begin composing digital poems, we can purposefully extend these concepts to develop students' growing knowledge about creating poetry. We can teach students to build on their imagery, for example, by adding pictures from the platform or uploading photos to augment their words. Students can enhance the mood of the poem through the power of music, matching the emotion they are trying to evoke through song and sound. Figure 5.5 shows some of the key lessons we might teach within a unit of study and the ways we might teach students to build on them in their digital clubs.

Figure 5.5
Key Unit Lessons and Digital Extensions

Unit of Study	Key Lessons for the Unit	Possible Digital Extensions of Key Lessons
Poetry	Poetry is built on the three pillars of emotion, imagery, and music.	• How to add images within the platform and upload personal photographs • How to add music within the platform
Argument Essays	• Opinions must be supported with evidence. • We can support our opinions with text evidence, facts, statistics, and quotes.	• How to find and choose powerful copyright-free images • How to add short video clips to your public service announcement • How to add narration to your announcement
Procedural Texts	Writers must provide clear step-by-step directions to the reader.	• How to add images and text to each step • How to add narration to each step
Fiction	Stories follow a plot structure and have key elements such as characters, setting, a problem, and a solution.	• How to choose characters and a background for your story (these choices might influence the story you write) • How to change background and images to follow your plot • How to add narration to your storybook • How to create a digital illustration

Figure 5.5 (continued)
Key Unit Lessons and Digital Extensions

Unit of Study	Key Lessons for the Unit	Possible Digital Extensions of Key Lessons
Informational Text	Informational writers use a variety of nonfiction text features to teach readers, including captions, labels, a glossary, and an index.	• How to make text features interactive by adding links to other websites and videos • How to add narration to domain-specific vocabulary to define it • How to find copyright-free images for your text
Book Reviews	Reviewers include a summary of the book and their opinion.	• How to add images from the platform or copyright-free images from the Web to your book trailer • How to add music to your video • How to create a QR code to link your trailer to the book

Letting the Digital Take the Lead

We also add in lessons showing how the program or application can lead the writing. We know that once students begin using a platform, the platform will sometimes impact what they create. For example, in our poetry unit, we suggest students begin by taking a poem they've written and digitizing it; however, we know once students log in to a platform and see some of the images available, they may instead choose an image and write a new poem based on that. As always, we keep in mind that writing is a process of creation and discovery, so this shift is expected, encouraged, and shared. We let our students share their discoveries with the group during minilessons, midworkshop teaching points, and the wrap-up.

Part Three: Clubbing Through Digital Clubs

Figure 5.6 shows an example of how digital complement clubs were added to a poetry study in a fourth-grade class. Please keep in mind that if the club meeting box is empty, there is no meeting during writing. If the box states writing time, students are writing as usual in workshop.

Figure 5.6 Sample Poetry Unit with Digital Complement Clubs

Grade: __4__   Unit: _Poetry_____   Timeframe: _Five Weeks_____

	Day 1:	Day 2:	Day 3:	Day 4:	Day 5:
Minilesson	Reading like a writer to explore poetry as a genre	Reading like a writer to explore poetry as a genre	Immersion: trying out poetry	The three pillars of poetry	Idea generation: writing from the heart
Writing and Conferring	Poetry try-its	Poetry try-its	Blackout poems	Finding examples of imagery, emotion, and music in mentor texts	Heart maps
Club Meeting					
Wrap-Up	Whole-group share: creating an anchor chart that lists key elements from the genre	Whole-group share: adding to the anchor chart from day 1	Sharing of blackout poems in small groups	Students share examples of the pillars they found in our poetry books	Museum share of heart maps
	Day 6:	Day 7:	Day 8:	Day 9:	Day 10:
Minilesson	Drafting poems	Adding rhythm to poetry through line breaks and white space	Adding rhythm to poetry with repetition	Adding imagery using similes and metaphors	Adding imagery using personification
Writing and Conferring	Writing fast and long from a heart map idea	Drafting poems and experimenting with rhythm	Drafting poems and experimenting with adding rhythm	Drafting poetry and experimenting with imagery	Drafting poetry and experimenting with imagery
Club Meeting					
Wrap-Up	Partner share of poems	Sharing drafts with partners	Sharing drafts with partners	Quaker share of favorite line from a poem	Partner share of favorite imagery in a poem

Figure 5.6 (continued)
Sample Poetry Unit with Digital Complement Clubs

	Day 11:	Day 12:	Day 13:	Day 14:	Day 15:
Minilesson	Introduce and immerse students in digital poetry	The basics: how to use the platform	Using your notebook to choose an idea for a digital poem	Finding and adding images to a digital poem	Adding audio to your poem through voice-overs
Writing and Conferring	Students study digital poetry examples	Students play with the platform	Students play with the platform and begin creating poems	Students try adding images to their poems	Students try adding audio to their poems
Club Meeting			Initial club meeting where students create club basics and discuss their plans for creating a digital poem		Students share their first digital poems
Wrap-Up	Group creates an anchor chart that lists key elements from digital poems and compares it to the chart regarding traditional poems. How are they the same? How are they different?	Students self-reflect on writing digital poetry and using the platform	Clubs pair up and share plans	Students share tips and tricks for using the platform with the group	Clubs pair up and share poems

	Day 16:	**Day 17:**	**Day 18:**	**Day 19:**	**Day 20:**
Minilesson	Staying with a comparison in a poem	Specificity in word choice to add imagery to poems	Using five-sense language to add imagery to poems	Adding real photographs to digital poems	Make a club or student famous for discovering a tip, trick, or technique for using the platform
Writing and Conferring	Writing time	Writing time	Writing time	Writing digital poems	Writing digital poems
Club Meeting				Feedback on digital poems	Feedback on digital poems
Wrap-Up	Partner share drafts	Partner share drafts	Quaker share of favorite line with imagery	Club members make plans based on feedback	Club members make plans based on feedback
	Day 21:	**Day 22:**	**Day 23:**	**Day 24:**	**Day 25:**
Minilesson	Revising poems by lifting a line	Revising poems by experimenting with line breaks and white space	Revising digital poems using all we've learned about writing poetry	Editing poems by playing with punctuation and font choices	Sharing and celebrating poetry with parents in our annual poetry café
Writing and Conferring	Revising poems	Revising poems	Revising digital poems	Editing digital and traditional poems	
Club Meeting			Feedback on revisions	Feedback on revisions and editing	
Wrap-Up	Sharing revisions with partners	Sharing revisions with partners	Sharing revision tips	Sharing editing tips	

SAMPLE CLUB WORK

Figure 5.7
Digital Poetry
Samples

Figure 5.7
Digital Poetry
Samples

LIFE AFTER DIGITAL CLUBS

As we mentioned at the beginning of the chapter, we like adding digital clubs to our units because they increase student engagement and allow for an expanded audience for kids' work. After digital clubs conclude, it is not uncommon for students to want to continue writing digitally. This adds an increased sense of purpose when students have access to computers as they shift from gaming to creating content. Students often continue creating poems, book trailers, or public service announcements long after the club is over and seek out new audiences for their work. We enjoy helping them find ways to share their work with a broader audience through the class's blog or the school's social media accounts. Receiving likes or comments from people outside the school walls is highly motivating for all students.

Section III

Stand-alone Clubs

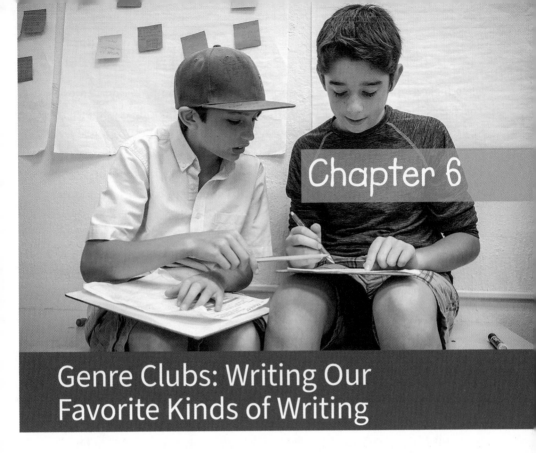

Chapter 6

Genre Clubs: Writing Our Favorite Kinds of Writing

G enre clubs are always one of students' favorite stand-alone units. A genre club is a small group of writers who are studying and writing in the same self-selected mode of writing. Genres that make great clubs include poetry, procedural texts, nonfiction books, graphic novels, memoirs, joke books, and series books, just to name a few. Kids love them because they're able to explore some of their most beloved genres, such as graphic novels and series books. Because this type of club is so popular, we suggest launching it early in the school year to generate enthusiasm for writing over the rest of the year.

Genre clubs aren't just a favorite club with students—teachers love them, too, and often comment that their kids write more during genre clubs than at any other time. In these clubs, students are highly engaged with their work, which builds stamina and fosters volume. We have watched many reluctant writers burn up the pages and produce large amounts of writing during this beloved club. The kinds of writing kids have often had to sneak around to do is now validated. How many of us have picked up a student's notebook only to find a comic hidden among the pages? In genre clubs, things like comics, fan fiction, or superhero stories are legitimized and encouraged. Celebrating these often overlooked genres is akin to what Linda Gambrell (1996) calls "blessing the book" in reading. Teachers bless a book by reading it aloud or doing a book talk about it, which makes the text more appealing to students. Gambrell suggests teachers work to bless lots of different genres, so every student can find books they love. Just as we work to bless all kinds of genres so every student falls in love with reading, we need to work to bless all kinds of genres, so every child becomes enamored with writing, too.

PREPARING FOR GENRE CLUBS

Before jumping into genre clubs, we need to do a few things to ensure this popular club runs smoothly.

Gathering Materials

One of the great things about writing clubs is that gathering materials can be a collaborative effort! For genre clubs, your main materials are books and typical writing tools. We suggest you choose high-interest books for your reveal. Though we prefer print-based texts, these books can be digital. As far as storing books, we use plastic bins from the dollar store or create a folder or collection in the digital ereading site.

Once students start clubs, they also spend some time envisioning the writing they will do and the materials they will need to do this writing. For example, in a comic book club, students will be drawing comics. Therefore, they would need paper with boxes for the comics and colored pencils or markers for drawing. Students often create paper templates, and we make copies for them.

Envisioning How the Work Will Go

Before you start, you will want to begin to gather texts and imagine the teaching possibilities around these texts. Remember: you will not do all of the research and gathering for this study. Just like in other clubs, students can and should be invited to help gather texts and materials for their chosen genre.

Another consideration is the audience. In many classrooms, a discussion of audience seems to be left until students are at the end of the writing process. As writers, however, we realize the importance of knowing your audience from the beginning—it gives purpose to our writing and influences every decision we make from idea generation, to drafting, to editing. For these reasons, we suggest discussing audience options for genre clubs early on. For example, if students decide that they will eventually make copies of their books and share them with a neighboring first-grade class, this decision affects everything from their choice of topic, to their characters, to their methods for illustrating, and their attention to editing. As it is with all things in writing clubs, students are an integral part of making this decision. We offer a few options for bringing students' writing into the world and let the groups determine others. Ultimately, it is the group who chooses how they will share their writing. In Figure 6.1, we offer a few suggestions for ways to make students' genre club writing public.

Figure 6.1
Publishing/Audience Suggestions for Genre Clubs

Publishing/Audience Suggestions for Genre Clubs
Reviews. Post reviews around the community or school: restaurant reviews at the local eatery, movie reviews at the local theater, video game reviews at the local gaming store, and book reviews at a bookstore or school library.
Graphic Novels/Comics. Create for a younger class, set up a day to share and then give copies to the kids, donate to the library, or sell copies to raise money for a charity.
Procedural Texts. Invite another class to read and try out the procedural text (make jewelry, origami, or paper airplanes).
Series Books or Other Forms of Fiction. Submit writing to literary magazines or participate in nanowrimo (https://nanowrimo.org); read series books to younger-grade students, and add these books to their classroom libraries.
Poetry and Songs. Poetry slam, poetry café, open-mic event where poetry and songs are performed and shared.
Nonfiction: Who Would Win? Books. Read-and-debate events: readers read the texts, choose a "side" based on their reading, partner up with a person from the opposite side, and debate using the facts shared in the texts.

When Will Genre Clubs Happen?

Genre clubs make a great stand-alone unit of study. They are the perfect antidote to the monotony of same-genre units. Even though genre units are a staple in our year, if we are always mandating the genre students write, they never show us all that we have taught them. In addition, providing students with a choice will give them agency over their writing in ways that other units of study do not.

Teaching Points to Consider

When we suggest teachers open up their curriculum to include genre clubs where every child is writing a different kind of piece, many become anxious. Teachers wonder how they will plan lessons that meet students' needs when they are writing a wide variety of genres. This concern has merit. In traditional units of study, every child is creating the same kind of writing, so planning lessons seems easier. How do we plan whole-group lessons to support students when they are all writing different kinds of things? We have found it's relatively simple if we keep one thing in mind: we must teach lessons that can apply to all writing, no matter what type. Some lessons that apply to all kinds of writing include:

- How to discover an idea by studying mentor texts
- How writers reread and revise as they compose
- How to collaborate with a peer on a piece
- How to determine a focus or a message
- How specificity improves word choice

We could go on and on, but we think we've made our point. If you were around as we were twenty-five years ago, our writing workshops were a place where all students were writing lots of different types of text each day. Some students wrote poetry, some wrote informational books, and some wrote narratives. Though this sounds like a recipe for disaster, it wasn't. We simply taught lessons on the things all writers need to know— things that aren't content specific. When you embrace this idea, planning mini-lessons in genre clubs no longer seems difficult.

CLUB TIME

One thing we love about writing clubs is the originality of the work. Every stand-alone club offers new challenges and opportunities for the students and teacher, and these challenges breathe new life into the writing classroom. This is especially true with genre clubs.

Part One: Forming and Launching Clubs

Because the launch of any club is designed to get students excited and ready to write, we suggest launching genre clubs as you complete a current unit of study in writing. For example, as students are editing and putting the final touches on their published pieces in the final days of a unit, you might decide to do minilessons to launch your new club. We have also had success borrowing a few minutes across the day from various subjects so we can have a twenty- or thirty-minute block for a few days. In this way, you keep students' writing stamina going and build excitement for what's to come.

We envision that you will need about twenty to twenty-five minutes a day for two or three days. A few things you will want to consider doing as you launch include:

- Revealing the upcoming club
- Allowing students to preview and pick their clubs
- Getting students to make plans for their upcoming club work

We have described how some of these lessons might go in the rest of this section.

The Big Reveal and Preview: Discovering Our Choices in the Unit of Study

Revealing genre clubs to students is exciting! Students love the idea of writing in a favorite genre with their peers by their side. One of the primary goals of the reveal is to get students excited about their upcoming club work. We build excitement for genre clubs by bringing in high-interest mentor texts that represent the genres students know and love. We also ask students two important questions:

- What genres do we love to read?
- What genres do we love to write?

The students and the teacher create a list of beloved genres and work to gather samples of each. As students are collecting texts, we remind them that each tub needs quite a few books for it to become a viable option. Students in one classroom scoured the teacher's library and visited the school library. They went to other classrooms in their hallway, asking those teachers to lend them books. They searched their homes to see what they could gather. We recommend about eight to ten mentor texts per tub because this allows every student to have two or three texts to study and share.

Once the genres are narrowed down to a few solid choices, we offer students a chance to take a closer look at their options by using a "speed-dating" approach, similar to what we do at the beginning of the year when students are searching for well-matched partners. In this case, we place the bins of books around the room. Students make their way around the room from bin to bin until every child has had a chance to look through each genre. To ensure things move at a steady pace, we set a timer and allow students five to seven minutes to study the texts. As students "speed-date," they take notes about every genre and their thoughts about writing it. Figure 6.2 is an example of the form we provide students during the speed date.

Figure 6.2
Genre Club Speed-Dating Form

Genre	What do I notice about this kind of writing?	Would I like to study/write this kind of writing for a while?	Genre Ranking

After students have had a chance to speed-date all the genres, they turn their forms in, and we use this information to create clubs. As we place students in clubs, our first consideration is the writing: we want students to be working in a genre they want to write. Our second consideration is social: we want students to work with compatible peers. We use all we know about students to create clubs where every member will feel valued, and we make sure to place all the students in one of their top genre choices.

Launching Genre Clubs: One Classroom's Journey

The first day Patty launched genre writing clubs in her fourth-grade classroom, she was both nervous and excited. She knew she wanted to provide time and space for students to be able to choose the genre of their writing, but she wondered if she would be able to manage the workshop. After all, workshop already feels a bit like herding cats. Would having students write in so many different genres make workshop feel truly unmanageable? She didn't know how it would go, but she knew she wanted to give it a shot.

She decided to start simple with a focus on bringing student choice and voice into the unit from the get-go. She let students know that they would be writing different texts and asked them to name the genres they loved to read and write (students had previously studied various genres, so they were familiar with the concept). Patty's conversation went something like this:

> *Patty:* Writers, today is an exciting day! I know that many of you have been asking me what our next unit of study is going to be, and I have been a little vague about it. Well, our next unit is going to be a new one—one where you are going to have a lot of time and space to work on something you love.

She looked around her meeting area and could see that students were both excited and curious. They kept looking around at each other to see if someone else knew what she was talking about. After about twenty or thirty seconds of looking around and nodding at each other, they turned back to her and she continued.

> *Patty:* We have been collaborating around books in our reading clubs, and I want to bring that element into writing. Our whole unit is going to be about "clubbing," but this time, as writers. And our clubs will be genres.

Students started talking at once, and she gave them the signal to listen up and continued talking.

Patty: This writing unit is going to be a little different. We won't all be writing in the same genre, but we will be writing in the same genre as other writers. We are going to form writing clubs based on the kind of texts we will be writing.

Immediately, Millie asked, "Can we choose the writing?" And Jordan followed up, "Can we write a piece with someone else?" And then Naomi, always the pragmatist, asked, "What will the minilesson be if we all are writing different texts?"

Patty chuckled at both their curiosity and their ability to get to the heart of the matter.

Patty continued: All good questions, my writing friends. We are going to choose the genre and, of course, the topic we want to write. We will still do our own writing pieces, but we will have LOTS of time to plan, study, and get feedback from other writers. And Naomi, well, that is a good question. Our minilessons will be on topics that apply to all of us—things we have studied this year or last, minilessons such as exploring writing, studying a mentor, choosing a seed, providing feedback that feels helpful, and engaging our readers. However, I will do small-group lessons with each club that will help support the specific elements of your genre.

And then David, always the cheerleader, asked, "Well, when do we get started?"

Patty continued: Well, writers, we are getting started today. And the way we will get started is by asking ourselves the following questions:

- What genres do we love to read?
- What genres do we love to write?

The students named quite a number of genres, from the more typical, traditional genres studied in school to forms and genres that students loved to read and write but had no opportunity to publish in school. Here is the original list:

- Letters
- Poetry
- Nonfiction (Students named features articles, how-to texts, all-about books, contest books)
- Realistic fiction
- Historical fiction
- Joke books
- Songs
- Reviews
- Mysteries
- Comics

She looked at this exciting but large list of texts and decided to pare it down. She asked them what genres they felt they wanted to write right now and what genres they had or could easily gather samples of to serve as mentor texts. The list was pared down to:

- Poetry
- Fiction (realistic and historical)
- Nonfiction (all-about and contest books)
- Reviews
- Comics

What was interesting about the list is that some of the genres are ones that students study over and over in their elementary school career, and others they have never studied or written. That said, this list is one that is manageable and, more important, inclusive of what writers wanted to study in clubs in the next few weeks.

Patty went on to conduct a genre-tasting experience where students would speed-date the genres. To recap, the steps to launch genre clubs follow:

1. Introduce the concept of clubs by asking students to consider the text types they love to read and write; create a large and inclusive list. Pare down the list to a manageable number of genres you can realistically find examples of and support.

2. Ask students to "speed-date" various genres and to rank their genre preferences. Use this information, and your knowledge of students, to create clubs.

Once the students are in their club, they need to prepare for their upcoming work. Some of the things we ask students to do to prepare for genre clubs include:

- **Naming Their Club.** We may have more than one club studying the same genre, so rather than calling them the Joke Book Club 1 and 2, we ask students to name their club. Naming their club is fun for kids and adds another layer of excitement to the work. The names are written on an index card and taped to the outside of the tub.

- **Collecting More Books.** Now that they are part of a club, students will need to examine the materials in their club's tub and determine whether they have enough or if they need to collect more. We suggest that each club have at least two books per child. We like four members in a club because we have found this fosters the most social interaction. When groups get larger than that, we often find one or two students disengaged during times of collaboration and feedback. Each tub should have from eight to ten texts for students to study and use as mentor texts. To gather more materials, we ask students to visit the school and class library again or to bring texts from home.

Part Two: Lessons

When planning lessons to support genre clubs, we consider what we know as writers: the value of studying mentor texts and experimenting with a genre. Before we write anything—a blog post, an article, a letter of recommendation—we immerse ourselves in the genre first to try it on.

We read and study a few mentor texts before drafting to become familiar with the kind of writing we will soon do. Katie Wood Ray writes, "Before revision, vision" (2006, 35). We believe reading and writing are two halves of the same whole; therefore, we ask students to do the work of real writers and immerse themselves in the genre by studying their club's mentor texts before putting pen to paper. This close reading and studying helps them become familiar with the overall structure and unique features of that type of writing. Therefore, we conduct lessons in the following:

- Reading like a writer
- Writing try-its

Reading Like a Writer

We have found it helpful to teach students a simple protocol for studying mentor texts, one that they can use in writing groups or anytime they want to closely examine a text or "read like a writer" (Ray 1999). The protocol we use has three steps: notice, name, and note (Eickholdt 2015).

■ **Noticing, Naming, and Noting.** We encourage students to study mentor texts throughout the writing process. However, in this first time through, we ask them to examine their text sets with a wide lens, seek-

ing out the bigger ideas associated with the genre. Later, we expect students to zoom in more closely and study individual texts to help them generate ideas, learn specific craft moves, and study writing techniques of various authors.

■ **Noticing.** Studying mentor texts begins with noticing. In this step, we ask students to look across all their books and notice the distinguishing features of the genre. We want students to understand that though "writing is individual, it is not unique" (Ray 1999). What we notice in one piece of writing can be found in other texts, and more important, this technique has a name.

■ **Naming.** It has been said that recognition leads to replication. We agree; naming is a powerful part of all learning, especially in writing. When we name something, it makes it repeatable. Once students notice a specific element that is unique to their genre, they give it a name. We encourage students to come up with their own labels for things—knowing literary terms is not critical. When students invent names for the things they observe, we know that it will be kid friendly and easier to remember. If we want kids to replicate the elements of a genre, they must label them, and they need to consider why they're important. Some elements of a genre might include speech and thought bubbles in comics, captions and close-ups in nonfiction, and stanzas and line breaks in poetry.

■ **Noting.** As a final step in the protocol, we ask students to note why the authors would include that element in their work. In other words, why is it important to the genre? Why is it noteworthy? Writers don't randomly do things as they write; instead, everything is done with purpose. Most often the purpose is because it will help the reader in some way. Considering what's best for the reader is an important part of being a writer. To support students as they notice, name, and note, we ask them to fill out the form in Figure 6.3.

Figure 6.3
Notice, Name, and Note Form:
Students' Observations of Joke and Riddle Books

Notice: What do we notice about the genre?	Name: What might we call it?	Note: Why is it important? How does it help the reader?
The books are about one thing, like holidays.	Theme	Readers like to pick out books about topics they are interested in.
Joke/riddle at top of the page, answer upside down on the bottom.	Upside-down answers	Lets the reader think about the answer before they see it.
Joke/riddle on one page, answer on the next page.	Hidden answer	Lets the reader think about the answer before they see it.

Writing Try-Its

During the beginning of genre clubs, as we immerse students in the new writing, we ask students to experiment and play around with the genre. This means that in their writer's notebooks, students will create snippets of writing in their chosen genre. These snippets are not necessarily full pieces or entries but playful and experimental examples of writing—we call these try-its. Try-its are just as the name implies—an opportunity to try out the genre and/or idea before committing to writing a complete piece. In fact, writers learn most from this kind of low-stakes writing, because it is an opportunity to experiment with the structure, form, and voice of writing before committing to an idea. During this stage, writers can:

- Experiment with various ideas, and explore where they lead
- Free-write in the genre
- Try two or three specific topics and decide which one wins and becomes the idea they will take through the process
- Imagine one scene or part from their writing and try it out
- Experiment with various leads

Another thing we love about genre clubs is how students become more in tune with their own unique writing processes. We encourage students to cycle through the process of composing at their own pace and in their own way, so they can discover what works for them. As they write, we support their work with lessons designed to support both process and craft.

Lessons to Support Writers as They Begin Writing in Genre Clubs

One of the most important things a writer needs is an idea. One of the simplest ways to generate ideas is to make a list. Because there's nothing like a new tool to spur on writing, we've had success by introducing students to small three-by-two-inch notebooks that are used specifically for catching ideas. These smaller notebooks are the perfect size for students to carry around in their pockets and use for jotting ideas whenever they come. In fact, a young writer in one of our former classes came up with this idea when she was struggling with remembering and capturing ideas.

She lamented this problem to the members of her memoir club, sharing how she would come up with ideas when she was at soccer practice or in the supermarket with her mother, only to forget them when she returned home or returned to school the next day. So, she whipped out a collection of small notebooks, one for each member of her club, so that like her, they could live like writers—always collecting ideas. Even when writers are away from their work, they are always thinking about it. By providing students with a place to capture their ideas, she—and now we (of course, we borrowed this great idea)—are helping them live a writerly life.

Because students get to choose the genre they want to study, we have found that unlike some of the other writing work we do, most students have lots of ideas they want to explore. If this is not the case, and you find students struggling to come up with things to write about, you might want to teach them some idea-generating strategies. This is where the mentor texts come in handy yet again. We ask students to peruse the books and ask, "What kinds of topics do you see that you might want to emulate?" Figure 6.4 shows one example of an anchor chart used by a third-grade graphic novel writing club.

Figure 6.4
Using Mentor Texts to Find Ideas in Graphic Novels

Genre	Mentor Text	Possible Idea Window or Possible Idea
Graphic Novels	*The Real Poop on Pigeons*	Wonderings and curiosities become writing topics
	Big Nate	Problems at school, friendship troubles
	Rebels	Historical events of interest make great ideas

Lessons to Support Students as They Draft

Once clubs are launched, most students will write with more zeal than they've ever written before. They'll be so enticed by the idea of writing their favorite type of text, they'll be burning up the pages with their pens. However, a few kids may not be as fluent and need some help getting their writing down. In the book, *Bird by Bird*, Anne Lamott (1995) calls the first stab at a piece "a shitty first draft." We obviously don't use the same nomenclature with kids, but we do try to convey the same message: the goal of drafting is to get something, even something messy, on paper. Writers need to know it's okay to write less-than-perfect first drafts because they will have plenty of time to go back and revise their writing later. The important thing is to have something to work on. So, it's important to teach students how to keep their mind and pencils moving.

Lessons to Support Students as They Work on Crafting Writing

Genre clubs create classrooms that are a hub of excitement. We often stand back and marvel at what's happening: students are happily writing, meeting with the members of their club for feedback and support, and writing some more. Their work has purpose, and this purpose brings engagement. Throughout genre clubs, we support students by teaching lessons to the whole group that help students improve the writing in any genre. Let's take a look at how a minilesson on improving the quality of students' club writing looked when Lisa taught it to a group of third-grade students. In this lesson, Lisa is teaching students the importance of including key elements of the genre. This lesson is important for all writers, no matter what kind of writing they are doing.

Lisa: Writers, at the beginning of our clubs, we studied examples of the kinds of text you all would soon write. Each club looked through their tub of mentor texts and practiced noticing, naming, and noting the things about their genre that made it special. You may remember that after you made your list of things you noticed, we went back in and thought about the M and Ms, or what *must* be in your piece and what *might* be in it (Coppola 2021). As you began writing, you wisely kept the "musts" and were sure to include them in your piece. Now as many of you are revising your work, I thought it would be a good idea to go back to the chart and consider the "mights." What else might we include that could make our piece stronger? Let me show you what I mean.

I've joined the All Stars. The All Stars are all working on comics, like me. I asked to borrow their chart, so I could look back through it to see some of the "mights." Let's take a look at their chart now. As you can see, they wrote *must* and *might* next to their entries. Some of their "musts" are boxes, speech bubbles, and thought bubbles. That makes sense—comics always have multiple boxes, and the character's use speech and thought bubbles. That's really what makes them comics, isn't it? Those are all a must. Now let's look at some of their "mights." I see they've listed a villain or nemesis as a might, different eyes for characters, and "pow" words. Okay, so I'm going to need some help from this group. I know what a villain is, but what are different eyes and "pow" words? What do they mean? Jose, can you explain these to me?

Jose: Sure. So, you know how you told us to just call what we notice anything? That the name didn't matter, as long as we knew what we meant?

Lisa: Yes. That's right. The name of the writing technique doesn't matter as long as your group knows what it means.

Jose: So, when we were studying the books, we noticed that a lot of times the character's eyes are different than regular eyes to show different things. Like when someone is in love their eyes become hearts, or when they're in a trance or being hypnotized or something, their eyes look like a circle with lots of lines like this (draws a curly cue on the board), or when they're dead, their eyes are Xs.

Lisa: Oh! Yes, I have noticed those different eyes. So, by just changing my character's eyes, I can show emotion or what's going on in the story. Interesting. I hadn't thought about that. Good idea. Hmmm . . . you got me thinking now.

Okay, what are "pow" words?

Jose: Well, sometimes the authors change the way the words look. They might make the letters really fat or change their shape or something. In a superhero story, when they're fighting or something, they might write, POW! And the letters are big and fat and stuff. See in this Superman story, where he's fighting the villain, *Kapow* is big and fat and the Os are like star-shaped. And in this book where the character is sleeping, they put a bunch of Zs with stripes, like the stripes on the character's pajamas.

Lisa: Oh, cool. So, the words are fancied up to add some more emphasis to the story. I see. Interesting. I hadn't thought about that.

So now after learning about the "mights" on this chart, I have some more ideas for what I could change in my story. I don't think I'll add a villain because I don't think it'd work in my writing, but I do think I'll try changing my character's eyes in a few places and adding some "pow" word shapes. I think those are two things that could really add a lot to my piece. Let me mark a couple places in my piece to remind me to make these changes (makes notes on her writing). Thanks for your help, All Stars!

Now it's your turn. I asked each club to bring their charts with them today for our minilesson. I want you to do what you saw me do with this chart. Read over it, and look at some of the "mights." Look through them and decide which ones you think you might want to try as you're revising your draft. Keep in mind, you get to choose—you don't have to use them all—but think about which "mights" you might want to try. Okay, turn and talk.

Lisa listens in as kids talk in their groups about the items on their charts and if and how they could use them.

Lisa: Okay, writers. I heard lots of great conversations today. Remember, as you revise your writing, adding some "mights" just might make it better! Before you leave the meeting area, please turn and tell your group your plans for writing today.

In addition to teaching whole-group lessons that apply to every kind of writing, we also teach small-group lessons that specifically apply to each club. For example, if students are writing poetry, we could pull them together and teach things like line breaks, white space, and stanzas.

Supporting Students at the End of the Club: Celebrating

All stand-alone clubs should end with a celebration. Students have spent weeks honing their writing craft in genre clubs. Though the work has been joyful, make no mistake—it has also been tough. To acknowledge students' hard work, a celebration is in order. In *Supporting Struggling Learners* (2017, 14), Patty writes:

> We have far too few celebrations in our classrooms, and celebration is key to moving struggling learners. Celebrate milestones, celebrate successes, and definitely celebrate hard work. I am not talking about "carrot and sticks" or any type of external reward, but a celebration of their work. Hard work is just that—hard to accomplish, but it will lead to success.

We mark the end of students' genre club journey with a class party. A few days before our party, we encourage students to spiff up their writing by adding details to their illustrations, creating covers for their books, and writing author bios. Then, we teach students the basics of merry-making. We discuss the things people do when they entertain guests, such as clean, decorate, and make or bring in food. Each group is given a small area to create their "party zone." Students get into creating decorations (the genres create a natural theme for each group's area) and bringing in food (students amaze us with all the food they will bring in for a celebration—we've never seen so many kinds of chips!). Many teachers enlist parent's help with classroom celebrations. Parents love creating genre-based food and decorations. We've had a Captain Underpants cake (Tra-La-Laaa), mystery cupcakes (magnifying glasses), and riddle cupcakes (question marks). We've also had parents donate balloons, posters, and confetti to help decorate each party zone. This is an exciting time, and parents are happy to help.

On party day, students rotate through each group's area, read their peers' writing, and basically have a great time. We make sure we provide students with lots of sticky notes to leave compliments on every writer's work. We love watching students beam as they read all the positive comments from their peers after the party is over. It's the perfect ending to one of our favorite clubs.

Part Three: Clubbing Through Genre Clubs

Figure 6.5 shows how a stand-alone genre club was implemented in one third-grade classroom. Please keep in mind that if the club meeting box is empty, there is no meeting during writing. If the box states writing time, students are writing as usual in workshop.

Figure 6.5
Genre Club Unit

Grade: 3	Unit: Genre Clubs		Timeframe: Four Weeks	
	Day 1:	**Day 2:**	**Day 3:**	**Day 4:**	**Day 5:**

	Day 1:	**Day 2:**	**Day 3:**	**Day 4:**	**Day 5:**
Minilesson	Reading like a writer: rereading our favorites to notice, name, and note key aspects of the genre	Studying key mentor texts for ideas	Developing theories about the genre	Studying the craft moves in genres: What must we include? What might we include?	Writing with a mentor text at your side
Writing and Conferring	Try-it writing	Try-it writing	Writing time	Writing time	Writing time
Club Meeting			Discussing theories developed regarding the genre	Establishing a list of musts and mights	
Wrap-Up	Notice, Name, and Note chart	Whole-group share of topics	Check-in: How is writing going?	Spotlight one club's work	Club share of crafting possibilities

	Day 6:	**Day 7:**	**Day 8:**	**Day 9:**	**Day 10:**
Minilesson	Write in the margins as a planning strategy	Keeping your pencil moving during drafting	Writing with your audience in mind	Studying text structures	Using precise words
Writing and Conferring	Writing time	Writing time	Writing time	Writing time	Writing time
Club Meeting			Who will we write for?	Feedback on ongoing drafts	

Figure 6.5 (continued)
Genre Club Unit

	Day 6 (cont'd):	Day 7 (cont'd):	Day 8 (cont'd):	Day 9 (cont'd):	Day 10 (cont'd):
Wrap-Up	Whole-class check-in: How's it going?	Sharing drafting tips and tricks	Clubs add audience possibilities to class chart	Club members share revision plans based off feedback	Clubs sit together and have a quick reflection conversation on first pieces
	Day 11:	**Day 12:**	**Day 13:**	**Day 14:**	**Day 15:**
Minilesson	Elaboration: how to add details to key parts of your piece	The end is just as important as the beginning: creating powerful endings	Playing with language: How might you use punctuation to guide the reader?	Back to the drawing board: more try-it writing based on personal goals	Begin at the beginning: How can you engage the reader from the start? What do writers in your genre do?
Writing and Conferring	Writing time	Writing time	Writing time	Writing time	Use moves from the Notice, Name, and Note chart to guide try-its
Club Meeting		Feedback on endings	Feedback on drafts		
Wrap-Up	"Sitting in the chair" protocol, whole group	Does your ending reflect your big idea?	Conventions share	Club goal share and reflections	Club reflections chart
	Day 16:	**Day 17:**	**Day 18:**	**Day 19:**	**Day 20:**
Minilesson	Using a checklist to revise	Revision: What do we leave in? What do we take out?	Editing for your audience. Who/where are you publishing your writing? How will this impact editing?	Polishing up one piece for celebrating	Writing celebration and club reflection

		Day 16 (cont'd):	Day 17 (cont'd):	Day 18 (cont'd):	Day 19 (cont'd):	Day 20 (cont'd):
Writing and Conferring			Writing time	Writing time	Writing time	Writing celebration and club reflection
Club Meeting		"Sitting in the chair" protocol using the writer's chosen technique against the club checklist	Show a student example of revision	*Clubs plan their celebration.*	*Clubs plan their celebration.*	
Wrap-Up		Three-minute quick share with each club	Partner share	*Clubs plan their celebration.*	*Clubs plan their celebration.*	

STUDENT SAMPLES

Figure 6.6
Student Comic Samples

Figure 6.6
Student Comic
Samples

LIFE AFTER GENRE CLUBS

Now that genre clubs have concluded, you may be wondering what to expect. As workshop teachers, our routine returns. This means we generally begin a new unit of study that often focuses around one genre for four to five weeks. But what happens with the students? As we mentioned at the beginning of the chapter, genre clubs breathe new life into the writing classroom. Students who were disengaged or avoiding writing in the past are now more engaged and even excited when we announce writing time each day. The one problem we have found is that students love genre clubs so much, they don't want to stop writing these pieces, which is a great problem to have! Now is the perfect opportunity to teach kids about keeping a side project (Cruz 2004). A side project is a piece of writing you work on when things aren't going well with your main writing or when you need a little break from your primary writing. As writers, we always have a few pieces going and move between them as we work. Keeping a side project is tremendously helpful when we get writer's block or become frustrated with one piece. We simply move to another and keep working.

We've also had success with dedicating time each week for what Ralph Fletcher calls "greenbelt" writing (Fletcher 2017). Greenbelt writing is low-stakes writing that allows students to explore and play. This writing is similar to the try-it writing we mentioned earlier in this chapter. We make time for greenbelt writing by giving kids the first few minutes of class each day (as students are arriving to class) or by dedicating one day a week of workshop to "freewriting." Low-stakes writing helps kids fall in love with writing, and this is important. When kids enjoy doing something, they do it more. When they do it more, they get better at it. We also believe that writing is something that makes life more meaningful and enjoyable. So, as we mentioned at the beginning of this chapter, helping kids fall in love with writing is a big goal of ours. Genre clubs help us reach this goal.

Chapter 7

Author Clubs:
Finding a Writing Mentor

As human beings, we all have favorites. We have favorite recipes, movies, songs and artists, places to go and visit, and even favorite people! The same can be true of students and the authors they love. Students have favorite books and favorite authors. Many have had them for years, since they were in preschool or kindergarten, and this was evident as they sat with rapt attention during read-aloud or quietly hunched over a book during independent reading. Author clubs look to capture that love—that ability to sit curled with a book or in rapt attention to the words—and use this power to learn from favorites.

Author studies have been around for years, as both reading and writing units, and have been making a recent resurgence in many classrooms. During a typical author study, the teacher and students study one author together, one they love, and they get to know that author well. In a reading author study, the purpose is to read many works by that author and to examine the craft as a reader. During this time, students develop the skill of analyzing writing as a reader and look to uncover how the decisions the author makes (use of text structures; literary elements, including characterization, plot, and setting; structure; perspective; language; genre choice; and even title) affects a reader and her understanding. In a reading author study, readers also have the opportunity to demonstrate their critique prowess by thinking critically about a text and then evaluating and sharing those opinions with evidence.

In a writing author study, the purpose is to read many works by an author and examine the craft as a writer. During this time, students develop the skill of analyzing writing as a fellow author and then earn their chops as an artisan. During the study, the teacher and students look to uncover the decisions a writer makes that influence a reader (use of focus, structure, elaboration, word choice, conventions) and to emulate those moves in their own writing.

For us, author clubs harness the power of all of that work, add in a layer of collaboration, and create an integrated unit grounded in student choice and agency. Our author club units:

- Create reading-writing connections
- Provide a context for real-world tasks and problem-solving opportunities
- Stand on the shoulders of giants and harness the power of "favorites"
- Provide choice of author—something not done in traditional author study units—which creates a sense of agency in our learners

Create collaborative opportunities for learning around discipline connections, authentic contexts, problem-solving opportunities, and use of mentors, choice, voice, and agency—these are why author clubs are critical to the development of students as writers and people. Plus, they are really fun!

PREPARING FOR AUTHOR CLUBS

As with any unit of study, it's helpful to begin by "getting ready" to implement the unit. This ensures that the clubs run smoothly and that you and your students feel ready for the exciting work ahead. We suggest that when you get ready for author clubs (and for any clubs, really) you do the following: gather materials, envision how the work will go, and consider the teaching points you will bring to your learners. Here is how it can go in an author club unit.

Gathering Materials

Author clubs, like all stand-alone clubs, employ the materials you are currently using in writing workshop and add a layer of novel, new items. You want to consider what authors your writers will study—children's literature today provides us with a plethora of choices. That being said, don't overwhelm yourself or your students with an enormous number of options. Consider what authors your students love and will willingly, and with gusto, sit beside their peers and this author for a few weeks. Figure 7.1, on the following pages, lists some of our favorites.

Envisioning How the Work Will Go

Before jumping into author clubs, we have a few things to do to ensure this popular club runs smoothly. You want to begin to gather texts and imagine the teaching possibilities around them. What qualities of good writing are evident? What does this author do especially well? Does this author provide students with windows, mirrors, or sliding glass doors (Bishop 1990)? Does the author create texts that will match student writing in kind, length, and/or form? Is this author someone who the students will gravitate toward and say, "I can do that, too!" What can this author teach the students to do better? They need to be someone whose writing students can emulate, someone close to their zone of proximal development (Vygotsky 1978).

It is important for teachers to remember not to do all the research and gathering for this study. Just as in genre clubs, students can and should be invited into this inquiry, gathering books and information about the chosen author.

Figure 7.1 Some Possible Authors for Author Clubs

Author and Titles	What Can This Author Teach Other Writers?	Which Grade Levels Might Be a Good Fit for This Author?
Matt de la Peña www.mattdelapena.com • *Last Stop on Market Street* • *Love* • *Carmela Full of Wishes* • *A Nation's Hope: The Story of Boxing Legend Joe Louis* • *Infinity Ring #4: Curse of the Ancients* • *Infinity Ring #8: Eternity* • *Ball Don't Lie* (YA novel) • *Superman* (YA novel) • *Mexican Whiteboy* (YA novel) • *We Were Here* (YA novel) • *Milo Imagines the World*	• Connection between experiences and topic choice: the power of telling your story • Rhythm and music of language • Sensory images • Word choice	Matt de la Peña is an author that grows with students. He has published picture books that are beloved by our early and middle elementary students, middle-grade novels for the engaging and unique Infinity Ring series, and YA novels on crucial and complex topics. Therefore, he is an author who is perfect for author clubs. If you are a teacher of students in grades three through five, the picture books and the Infinity Ring series are perfect for your students to read, love, and study. If you are a teacher of grades five through eight, we suggest using the picture book, *A Nation's Hope*, the Infinity series, and the YA novels listed to the left.
Jacqueline Woodson www.jacquelinewoodson.com • *The Day You Begin* • *Pecan Pie Baby* • *We Had a Picnic This Sunday Past* • *This Is the Rope* • *Each Kindness* • *The Other Side* • *Coming on Home Soon* • *Show Way* • *Harbor Me* • *Last Summer with Maizon* (trilogy) • *Brown Girl Dreaming* • *From the Notebooks of Melanin Sun* • *I Hadn't Meant to Tell You This*	• Connection between experiences and topic choice: the power of telling your story • Dialogue that expresses characters' emotion and voice • Sensory images • Sense of place in writing	Jacqueline Woodson is a prolific author who writes picture books, middle-grade chapter books, a memoir in verse, and YA novels and is now the author of an adult fiction book. If you are a teacher of students in grades three through five, the picture books and *Harbor Me* are perfect for your students to read, love, and study. If you are a teacher in grades five through eight, we suggest using the picture books and any of the middle-grade or YA chapter books that you feel are appropriate and resonate with your students.

Figure 7.1 (continued) Some Possible Authors for Author Clubs

Author and Titles	What Can This Author Teach Other Writers?	Which Grade Levels Might Be a Good Fit for This Author?
Jane Yolen https://www.janeyolen.com • *Letting Swift River Go* • *Water Music* • *Owl Moon* • *Encounter* • *Granddad Bill's Song* • The Dinosaur books • *The Devil's Arithmetic*	• Sensory images • Word choice, including sound words and repetition • Inside story through thoughts and feelings • Varied sentence length • Strong setting	Jane Yolen is the author of more than 300 books, representing a plethora of genres including poetry, memoir, and realistic and historical fiction. She is a writer we like to use to study how authors vary genre, use their own lives to write, use various techniques for gathering ideas, vary sentence length, and use dialogue. Jane Yolen is the perfect author for students in grades three through six.
Carmen Agra Deedy www.carmenagradeedy.com • *The Library Dragon* • *Martina the Beautiful Cockroach* • *The Last Dance* • *14 Cows for America* (http://14cowsforamerica.com) • *The Yellow Star: The Legend of King Christian X of Denmark* • *Growing Up Cuban in Decatur, Georgia* • *The Cheshire Cheese Cat: A Dickens of a Tale*	• Storytelling as a means of idea generating • Word choice • Show, don't tell via description • Varied sentence type (using descriptive phrases and compound and complex sentences)	A master storyteller who has been writing for children and young adults for more than two decades, Carmen Agra Deedy is the recipient of many awards by parents and organizations. Deedy's books give voice to hard moments and are varied in genre, form, and topic. A favorite of students in upper elementary and early middle school, Deedy is an ideal author club author.
Ezra Jack Keats https://www.ezra-jack-keats.org • *Peter's Chair* • *Apt. 3* • *The Snowy Day* • *Goggles!* • *Whistle for Willie* • *Pet Show* • *A Letter to Amy*	• Use of universal yet personal themes • Inside story through dialogue, thoughts, and feelings • Creating a character that is in more than one text	Ezra Jack Keats was an innovator ahead of his time who created books with diverse characters. He is a good writer to use to model how one writer writes many episodes for one character and is great for narrative studies and for illuminating dialogue and internal thinking. His books are beloved by students, and he is a great author to study the craft of writing in grades one through four.

Figure 7.1 (continued) Some Possible Authors for Author Clubs

Author and Titles	What Can This Author Teach Other Writers?	Which Grade Levels Might Be a Good Fit for This Author?
Eve Bunting https://www.scholastic.com/teachers/authors/eve-bunting/ • Secret Place • Train to Somewhere • Dandelions • The Wall • Smoky Night • Fly Away Home • A Day's Work	• Rhythm • Sound words • Imagery • Strong setting leads • Dialogue	Eve Bunting is a writer who can mentor us as we explore writing about important themes, using the page in interesting ways, creating a narrative text structure, and developing characters.
Patricia Polacco https://www.scholastic.com/teachers/authors/patricia-polacco/ • The Bee Tree • The Keeping Quilt • Pink and Say • Thunder Cake • My Rotten Red-Headed Older Brother • Thank You, Mr. Falker	• Reflective endings • Many moments and progressive narrative text structure • Word choice • Dialogue • Point of view • Strong setting • Internal thinking and character feelings	Patricia Polacco is a master storyteller who blends memory, observation, and imagination beautifully and can be used to study endings and story elements. She is an author who is well suited for author clubs in grades three through five.
Peter Brown www.peterbrownstudio.com • The Curious Garden • You Will Be My Friend • Mr. Tiger Goes Wild • Flight of the Dodo • The Wild Robot • The Wild Robot Escapes	• Telling a story in pictures and words • Use of long and short sentences for effect • Speech bubbles • Repetition • Strong setting leads • Stretching a scene with descriptive details	Peter Brown is not only the award-winner author of The Wild Robot and many other texts for students in grades one through five, but he is also an illustrator. This makes him a unique choice as the meaning making, in words and pictures, is done by the same person. Peter Brown has written both simple, yet engaging pictures books, as well as middle-grade chapter books that are beloved by many.

Figure 7.1 (continued) Some Possible Authors for Author Clubs

Author and Titles	What Can This Author Teach Other Writers?	Which Grade Levels Might Be a Good Fit for This Author?
Eloise Greenfield https://www.harper collins.com/ author/cr-100356/ eloise-greenfield/ https://www.poetry foundation.org/poets/ eloise-greenfield • *Honey, I Love and Other Poetry* • *Childtimes: A Three-Generation Memoir* • *For the Love of the Game: Michael Jordan and Me* • *In the Land of Words* • *The Great Migration: Journey to the North*	• Telling a story in poetry and as a narrative • Use of memory, observation, and imagination to generate ideas • Rhythm and rhyme • Word choice	Eloise Greenfield is a writer who is a master at sound, rhythm, and using various structures in writing. She writes in many genres. Eloise Greenfield is well-suited to author clubs in grades three through five.
Steve Jenkins http://www.stevejenkins books.com • *Actual Size* • *Who Am I?* • *What Do You Do with a Tail Like This?* • *Creature Features* • *Look at Me!*	• Creative use of the page to convey information • Comparisons • Partner facts • Print effects (italics, bold, larger print size)	Steve Jenkins is a master of nonfiction writing. He uses comparisons, creates images, and gives the reader an array of intriguing information. He is a great author club author for students in grades three through five.
Seymour Simon http://www.seymour simon.com • *Dogs* • *The Moon* • *Guts* • *How to Talk to Your Computer* • *Einstein Anderson: Science Geek* (series)	• Author-authority connection • Word choice • Conveying information via description • Conveying information via action facts	Seymour Simon is a nonfiction author who writes on a plethora of topics that interest students in grades three through six. His literary nonfiction is written with authority, nicely blending expository text with voice. Simon has books written in both English and Spanish.

Figure 7.1 (continued) Some Possible Authors for Author Clubs

Author and Titles	What Can This Author Teach Other Writers?	Which Grade Levels Might Be a Good Fit for This Author?
Cynthia Rylant www.simonandschuster.com • *When I Was Young in the Mountains* • *The Relatives Came* • *The Great Gracie Chase* • *In November* • *Night in the Country* • *The Wonderful Happens* • *Best Wishes* • *Waiting to Waltz* • The Henry and Mudge series • The Cobble Street Cousins series • *Rosetown* • *Every Living Thing* • *A Fine White Dust* • *The Van Gogh Cafe* • *I Had Seen Castles*	• Uses her life and her experiences as ideas and inspiration • Repetition • Use of various text structures (chronological, many moments, circular) • Sensory images • Word choice • Varied sentence structure	Cynthia Rylant is the author of more than 100 books for children, spanning early chapter books to early- and middle-grade picture and chapter books, to short stories and YA poetry collections. Rylant is an author who grows with children by writing about topics and themes that resonate with them across their elementary and middle school years.

When Will Clubs Happen?

In Chapter 2, we provided options for how writing clubs can fit into the existing fabric of writing time. As we explained, clubs can happen in two ways: as a complement to another unit of study (integrated and threaded throughout) or as a stand-alone unit. Author clubs can be either but make a perfect stand-alone unit of study. First, they provide a natural opportunity to integrate many of the components of language arts: reading, writing, speaking and listening, and even some language conventions. Moreover, author clubs are the perfect antidote to the monotony of genre units. Genre units are a staple in our year, but we want to punctuate the year with various pause points for other units of study, and an author club is the ideal unit to do just that. See Chapter 1 Figures 1.4 and 1.5

for two examples of where to conduct author clubs within a year of writing instruction.

Teaching Points to Consider

Author Clubs are opportunities to study both the craft and life of authors the students choose themselves. Rather than study the craft of writing only in genre units, author units allow teachers to provide lessons in craft and technique and allow students the opportunity to practice the craft of writing in self-selected topics and genres—ones that connect to and represent the author they are studying. Figure 7.2 describes teaching points that can be taught in an author club unit.

Figure 7.2
Teaching Points to Consider in an Author Club Unit

Teaching Point	Tips for Implementing
Writers read widely around an author and notice what the author does well. We call this reading like a writer. Today I am going to teach you how to read with a writing craft lens.	• Select a "class author" for your demonstrations during minilessons. This works best if your students are familiar with this author. • Provide each club with three to five titles from their chosen author. Multiple copies of texts, print or digital, are a plus.
Writers don't just read books by their chosen author, they also research the author's life, including their childhood and writing habits. Today I am going to teach you how to use (an author's website, article on the author, dedication page) to research the life of your club author.	• Provide students with author websites. You can also find information on various authors on publishers' websites (Scholastic, Penguin, etc.). • Check to see if author information is published in a book, such as in the Meet the Author series and the Author at Work series by Richard Owen Publishers. • Alert students to the About the Author or dedication pages of a book. Often, you can find information about an author and their life there.

Figure 7.2 (continued) Teaching Points to Consider in an Author Club Unit

Teaching Point	Tips for Implementing
When reading like a writer, reading about your chosen author's life, or reading to notice and name craft techniques, it is helpful to read closely and ask questions. This will help you build a theory about the author as a writer and, in turn, be able to use what you have learned in your own writing. Today I am going to teach you how to do a close read of a section of text and ask questions that will enable you to know your author deeply.	• Provide students with questions to ask. They can include: – What are common topics/ideas, themes, or lessons in this author's books? – Are there recurring characters or elements of plot? – What elements and craft techniques do I like best as a reader and a writer? – Where did the author get the idea for this piece of writing? – How might the author use their folder/notebook? – Which author(s) might have served as a mentor for this author? – Why did the author choose to write this piece? – How did the author develop/craft this writing piece? – How and where was this piece published?
When writers are studying a mentor writer, they create a chart of their noticings. Today I am going to teach you how to create an author's craft chart of noticings.	• Teach students to notice, name, note, connect, and envision the writing craft the author uses (Ray 1999). See Figure 7.3 for more ideas about how to create an anchor chart in an author club unit.
When moving from studying an author to writing like an author, it helps to compare yourself to the author—how you are alike and different—and then set writing goals. Today I am going to teach you how to move to writing like your author club author by first asking what your author understands and uses and then asking which of those habits, processes, or craft techniques might work for you as a writer.	• Use the author craft charts to find moves and techniques to emulate. • Demonstrate this as a three-step process: – Compare myself to the author. – Notice and name comparisons and strengths. – Try moves!

Teaching Point	Tips for Implementing
It has been said that we don't learn by just doing—we learn by doing and reflecting on what we have learned. Today, I am going to teach you how to reflect on what you have learned so that we can own and celebrate our new learnings!	• Celebrate accomplishments! Never underestimate how important it is to acknowledge all of the try-it writing students have done and how much they have learned and grown as writers (and even readers!).

Figure 7.3
How to Create an Author's Craft Inquiry Chart

What to Do	How to Do It
Notice something about the author's craft.	• Focus on how the writing is done by reading like a writer. • Talk about/generate a list of author's craft noticings. • Jot an example of the craft technique.
Name the craft.	• Create and use student-created descriptive names that are single words or short phrases (e.g., partner facts). • If possible, use known literary terms or names (e.g., simile/metaphor, alliteration, personification).
Note why the author may have chosen a particular craft technique.	• Why did the author choose to do this? • Discuss why the author chose the move and why it is notable.
Try this craft in your own writing.	• Reflect on existing drafts/ideas for drafts: "What would this technique sound/look like if it were used in my writing?" • Emphasize choice of craft related to purpose: "If I am writing and I want to _____, then I can use this technique." • Model an oral rehearsal strategy known as "Writing in the air" using student writing: "If _____ wanted to try this with his piece on _____, he could write. . . ."

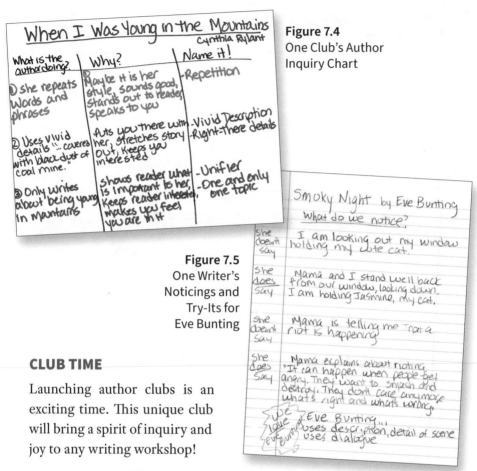

Figure 7.4
One Club's Author
Inquiry Chart

Figure 7.5
One Writer's
Noticings and
Try-Its for
Eve Bunting

CLUB TIME

Launching author clubs is an exciting time. This unique club will bring a spirit of inquiry and joy to any writing workshop!

Part One: Forming and Launching Clubs

Although we always try to live by Don Murray's adage, "Never a day without a line," we do see the value of taking just a bit of time to launch any stand-alone club. Therefore, we want to let students know not only what the next unit of study is but also the layer of choice in the unit of study. We can do this in the following places:

1. During a morning meeting

2. During the last twenty minutes of a writing workshop that precedes the onset of clubs

3. Flipped as a digital announcement in Google Classroom

The Big Reveal and Preview:
Discovering Our Choices in the Unit of Study

Revealing author clubs to students is exciting! Students love the idea of having a favorite author by their side during writing. One of the primary goals of the reveal is to get students excited about their upcoming club work. We build excitement for author clubs by bringing in high-interest mentor texts that represent authors they know and love and have been reading and studying this year (or even in prior years). Before deciding which authors we present to students in the reveal, we observe our students' reading habits and reflect on which authors have resonated with them. As we reflect, we ask questions such as:

- What authors are students currently reading?

- What authors do students seem drawn to when we visit the library?

- What authors do I know students of this age love?

- Are there any new authors I want to introduce to my kids?

- Which authors have texts that represent the qualities of writing I want my students to emulate?

When choosing authors, we also consider our overall writing curriculum, the genres we'll be teaching, and the mentor texts we have already used. See Figure 7.1 (earlier) for a list of our favorites.

Author clubs are the perfect place to reflect on reading-writing connections. Therefore, we want to launch and connect the study to the ongoing work of reading and writing workshops. We might begin an author study by saying:

Teacher: Friends, I've noticed that we love books by _____. In writing workshop, we have been working as writers. We have been generating new writing, going back to writing, and writing for a variety of reasons. In reading workshop, we have been working as readers, reading and finding books we love and that feel just right for us, setting reading goals, and reading and talking with partners. Well, readers and writers sometimes read and study one author together so that they can learn deeply from this writer.

So, for the next few weeks, we are going to read, reread, and look closely at one author with fellow learners who love this author. We will continue to love and spend time with this author and their books, but more important, we will learn new craft techniques to become better writers. Let's generate a list of authors we know and love and would want an opportunity to study.

In our own classrooms, and in the many classrooms where we have launched author clubs, we have executed a few different methods for revealing possible authors and choosing a club. The following models work well for in-person teaching, but they also work well if you are teaching in a hybrid, HyFlex, or remote setting:

1. **Author Tasting.** Similar to a book tasting, students have the opportunity to move around the room and remind themselves about this author. The teacher takes some of the suggested authors from the class-generated list and adds a few of her own choices to create stations around the room. Each station has a basket of books by that author, a device open to the author's webpage, and any anchor charts or other class materials related to the author. Students go around the room and spend five to ten minutes perusing books, surfing the author's website, and reminding themselves of what they love about this author. Students have an Author Club Speed-Dating Form (Figure 7.6) by their side as they "taste" the choices put forth for author clubs.

2. **Digital Sampling.** Similar to the author tasting, students have the opportunity to peruse author possibilities in a digital format. The teacher creates a digital collection, a digital bin, or a shelf in their Bitmoji classroom for each author. Students can then peruse the books by an author, read reviews, read and view the author's webpage, and interact with other students in a digital space (Padlet works great!) to sample the author club offerings. Just as in the author tasting format, students have the Author Club Speed-Dating Form (Figure 7.6) by their side.

In either format, students note their likes and preferences and rank their top three choices. In addition to listing which author they wish to study, they explain why. The teacher can then review the author forms and create author clubs that will work well for all learners in the class.

Figure 7.6
Author Speed-Dating Form

Name _____

Author	What I Notice/Like About This Author?	Would I Like to Study This Author? Why?	Author Ranking

One Team's Journey

As Patty was helping Joseph, Eleanor, and Mike launch clubs in their fourth-grade classrooms, she and the teachers noted that students were excited to begin author clubs. Because this was going to be a reading and writing unit (with both reading and writing goals, reading and writing minilessons, and implemented during both reading and writing workshops), this unit would be a big moment!

All three teachers opted for an author tasting for each of their fourth-grade classrooms, because they wanted students to interact with each other and with the possible authors in stations and jot notes on what they noticed about students. Kid-watching (Goodman 1985) is a powerful assessment protocol, grounded in observation and the belief that students demonstrate capacities, strengths, needs, and wants to us on a daily basis. Therefore, Joseph, Eleanor, and Mike were ever-present mentor readers and writers, ready to answer questions and write down observations as students moved in a speed-dating format from author station to author station.

This team of fourth-grade teachers had many conversations with both their literacy coach and with Patty about which authors to choose. They all have robust classroom libraries, promote daily independent reading, and read aloud frequently, so they had numerous authors from which to choose.

What was important to this team, and what has always been important to us, is to choose authors that provide students with many access points and the ability to read and study texts in high volume. Therefore, although many excellent authors exist for students at this grade level, it was essential to everyone that the author wrote short and long texts in multiple genres.

The author club choices for these students were Cynthia Rylant, Ezra Jack Keats, Eve Bunting, Carmen Agra Deedy, Peter Brown, and Eloise Greenfield. Each of these authors is quite prolific, writing across genre

and form, and is beloved by readers in these classes. They were the perfect array of choices to meet all student interests and needs.

On the first day of clubs, known as the launch day, students were eager to see what groups they would be placed in. Students gave their top three choices on the Author Speed-Dating Form, and Joseph, Eleanor, and Mike made every effort to put students into clubs of either their first or second choice. They placed the author baskets in the meeting area and created an index card with the names of the writers in each club.

On that first day, students had an opportunity to once again browse the books, make a plan for reading the texts, and set goals as writers.

Part Two: Lessons

Author clubs, like all stand-alone club units, are implemented as a unit of study, across a time frame that matches that unit. Units are generally four to five weeks, and the author club should fall in that range.

When planning lessons to support this club, we draw from Figure 7.7, which shows our chart representing the writing qualities taught in any unit of study. A similar chart also exists in Chapter 4.

Figure 7.7
Writing Qualities with Guiding Questions

Writing Qualities	Definition and Guiding Questions
Focus	Writing should focus on a moment, idea, or message. Focus is the most important quality because it affects everything else. Focus brings clarity to a piece. • What is the focus of this piece? Is it about an event, an issue, or big idea that the writer wants to share in writing? • How does the author convey their focus?
Structure	Structure refers to how the piece is organized or put together. Ideas should be grouped in meaningful ways, with important parts or events emphasized and unimportant parts or events excluded or deemphasized. Writing should flow from idea to idea in ways that are clear and accessible to the reader. • How does the writer organize the text? • What kind of text structure does the author use? • How does the writer draw you into the text via a lead, leave you with a satisfying ending, and transition from part to part?

Figure 7.7 (continued) Writing Qualities with Guiding Questions

Writing Qualities	Definition and Guiding Questions
Elaboration	Elaborating is often described as adding details or telling more. Writers elaborate by showing, not telling, or with explanation and example. Much of what we teach kids about writing well has to do with elaboration. If there is a key to good writing, elaboration is it. • How does the writer stretch out the heart of the story or expand on the most important parts? • What craft moves does the author use to help you envision the story? • What kind of facts does the author include in a nonfiction piece—action facts, partner facts, description facts? • What kind of evidence does the author provide for their argument? Where in the world can you find this kind of evidence?
Word Choice	Word choice paints a picture for the reader. It helps the reader envision people, places, ideas, concepts, and things and put themselves in the story, message, or concept. Careful word choice adds voice to a piece. • How does the author use words that are precise or specific to the content/topic? • How does the author paint a picture with words? What kinds of words does the author use to do that? (Striking adjectives, vivid verbs, lingo or discipline-specific words, or words from another language)
Conventions	Conventions make a piece easier to read. Intentional use of conventions can help the writer add voice to their piece. • How does the writer create stopping and pausing points and use punctuation to guide your reading? • What specific kinds of print and font treatments and punctuation does the author use? (Italics, bold, larger print size, placement on the page, use of ellipses, dashes, exclamation marks) • How does the author use sentence structure to engage you and guide the way you read? (Long and short sentences, appositive and introductory phrases, openers and closers, compound and complex sentences)

Figure 7.8
Sentence Stem Chart for Studying Author's Craft

Sentence Stems We Noticed Our Author Uses When Showing a Character's Internal Thinking	
• I thought...	• I wished ...
• I always wondered ...	• I worried that ...
• I noticed ...	• I was surprised by ...
• I suddenly realized ...	• I couldn't believe ...

Part Three: Clubbing Through Author Clubs

Here is one way an author club can go. This example is from a fourth-grade classroom, but the lessons and unit can be used with minor adjustments across grades three through six. In addition to minilessons about writing qualities, these units included minilessons in writing process and collaboration. Please keep in mind that if the club meeting box is empty, there is no meeting during writing. If the box states writing time in the box, students are writing as usual in workshop.

Figure 7.9
Author Club Unit

Grades: 3–6   **Unit:** Author Clubs   **Timeframe:** Four Weeks

	Day 1:	Day 2:	Day 3:	Day 4:	Day 5:
Minilesson	Reading like a writer: rereading our favorites to notice, name, and note our author	Authors are writers and people: studying the life of our mentor authors	Developing theories about the author by asking seminal questions	Creating an author checklist: create a club checklist of all the ways the club can write like the author	Studying the ways our author elaborates using internal thinking
Club Meeting			Club meeting, discussing theories around writing ideas and author's purpose		Club meeting

Figure 7.9 (continued) Author Club Unit

	Day 1 (cont'd):	Day 2 (cont'd):	Day 3 (cont'd):	Day 4 (cont'd):	Day 5 (cont'd):
Writing and Conferring	Writing time; teacher meets with clubs around the author, try-it writing	Writing time; teacher meets with clubs around the author, try-it writing	Writing time	Writing to discover: trying out our author's seminal moves	Writing time
Wrap-Up	Notice, Name, and Note chart	Notice, Name, and Note chart, adding information about the life and work of the author	Check in: How is writing going?	Make someone famous: idea and entry generating in the spirit of your author	Club Quaker share of a powerful line

	Day 6:	Day 7:	Day 8:	Day 9:	Day 10:
Minilesson	Write in the margins as a drafting strategy (to be used when writers are ready to draft)	Five-minute review of Notice, Name, and Note protocol	Considering audience: Who will we write for?	Studying structure: circular vs. chronological—what does your author use?	Revision strategy considering word choice: cracking open the idea by using precise words
Club Meeting		Study mentor texts, notice and name craft techniques to try			
Writing and Conferring	Writing time	Writing time	Writing time and midworkshop: giving a glow and a grow to fellow writers in our club	Writing time	Writing time and midworkshop: Quaker share/Read into the circle of vivid and precise language
Wrap-Up	Status of the class (Atwell 1987): Where are you and where are you going next?	Share author charts across clubs	Whole-class Quaker share/ Read into the Circle of a powerful line	Wrap-up/club time: provide feedback on entries/drafts written using the inspiration and techniques learned	Clubs sit together and have a quick reflection conversation

	Day 11:	Day 12:	Day 13:	Day 14:	Day 15:
Minilesson	Elaboration via Lift a Line: How to stretch the heart of your piece	The end is just as important as the beginning: studying our authors' endings	Playing with language: How does your author use pausing and stopping points to guide the reader?	Back to the drawing board: more try-it writing based on personal goals	Begin at the beginning: How does your writer engage the reader?
Club Meeting		Studying authors' endings	Studying author's use of pausing and ending punctuation		
Writing and Conferring	Writing time	Writing time	Writing time	Writing time	Use moves from the Notice, Name, and Note chart to lead try-its
Wrap-Up	Sitting in the Chair protocol, whole group	Does your ending reflect your big idea?	Conventions share	Club goal share and reflections	Club Advice Chart: see Figures 7.4, 7.5

	Day 16:	Day 17:	Day 18:	Day 19:	Day 20:
Minilesson	Using our checklist to revise: try a technique particular to your author	Revision: What do we leave in? What do we take out?	Editing for structure: Did I paragraph using PATS— place, action, time, speaker?	Publishing using the Author Club checklist	Writing celebration and club reflection
Writing and Conferring	Writing time	Writing time and midworkshop: make a student in the class famous by showing an example of someone leaving something unimportant out	Writing time	Writing time	

Figure 7.9 (continued) Author Club Unit

	Day 16 (cont'd):	Day 17 (cont'd):	Day 18 (cont'd):	Day 19 (cont'd):	Day 20 (cont'd):
Club Meeting	Sitting in the Chair protocol: using writer's chosen technique against the club checklist		*No official club time. Clubs may choose to meet.*	*No official club time. Clubs may choose to meet.*	Writing celebration and club reflection
Wrap-Up	Three-minute whip-around with each club sharing what is working well	Wrap-up	Checking up on our Author Club checklist	Preparing for celebration	

STUDENT SAMPLES

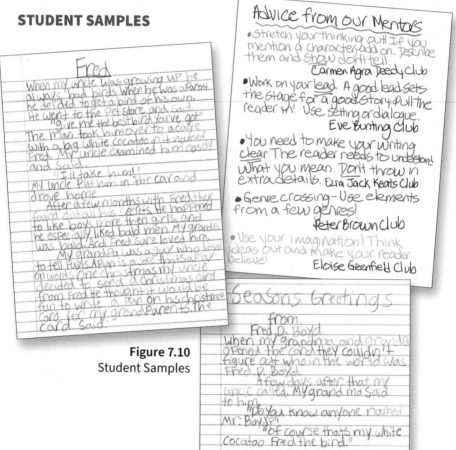

Figure 7.10
Student Samples

LIFE AFTER AUTHOR CLUBS

We have found that author clubs leave students with a renewed energy for writing! Students are empowered by their mentorship and by the autonomy and decision-making they engage in. We therefore suggest that regardless of where you go next, you continue this thread in other units. In particular:

- Always allow students to have a personal mentor in each unit of study. There will, of course, be the class mentors, but students now have a will and a way to have individual preferences be part of the fabric of any unit of study.

- Keep the qualities of writing alive! Keep Figure 7.7 by your side as you plan the whole-class, small-group, and individual teaching for future units of study. Even if you have a purchased or team-created unit of study, differentiate your teaching according to students' needs by tapping into our qualities chart!

- Keep engagement high by continuing on this road of student autonomy. Consider what choices students have in each unit, and look to create at least three places where students can determine their course of action.

- Keep low-stakes writing alive. This unit was grounded in lots of "try-it" writing—or writing that is not for the sole purpose of publishing—and writers really flourish when they have these opportunities!

Chapter 8

Conventions Clubs: Authentic Opportunities to Play with Writing

ere we are, at the final club chapter! At this point in your reading, you might be right there with us in the belief that writing clubs are an engaging and essential part of your writing year. You may have plans to implement a club or two in your year. You may have implemented a club already—stand-alone or complement—and you may have even implemented more than one.

All that being said, you might be wondering why our last club chapter is about conventions. Why take conventions and make it a club offering? And why a stand-alone offering? For us, the conventions of writing are not just a perfunctory task. Yes, our writing needs to be correct to go out into the world, and we too struggle with making sure our students know enough about how to do that. But that is not why we are such advocates of conventions clubs. We recommend this kind of club because it is an example of what we believe all clubs to be: opportunities for students to experiment and play with writing. As Ralph Fletcher (2017) would say, it's a *Joy Write* opportunity. What do we mean by that? Well, consider the first two paragraphs of this chapter. In paragraph one, we used the em dash to set apart the phrase "stand-alone or complement," because we felt it worked much better than using commas. Could we have used commas? Sure, they would absolutely be correct. But we did not. Why? Because we feel the sentence reads better. It provides the reader with a way to really hear our voice, one that if it were speaking to you would emphasize that phrase.

Still not convinced? Well, in the wise words of one of our conventions mentors, Jeff Anderson, grammar and conventions are just as much about style as they are about correctness. In *Mechanically Inclined* he writes,

> It's fair to say we don't often hear an encouraging, tolerant tone toward grammar and mechanics errors in society or in many classrooms. "Grammar and mechanics are to be done correctly or not at all" is more often the underlying message. What about experimentation? Play? Approximation? Grammar and mechanics shape meaning and as in all language endeavors, we must make mistakes to move toward correctness. Where's the bridge between getting started and stretching with grammar and mechanics and being wrong? (2005)

When we allow students to experiment and approximate, to find a need and desire to attend to the conventions of their writing, we have the best results. Our students will actually learn more about the rules of our language system, and when and where to use them correctly and artfully, when we allow them to learn via play and approximation.

Therefore, for us, conventions clubs:

- Provide a context for authentic conventions work

- Create a felt need for the writer to want to work on conventions

- Create collaborative opportunities for learning and growing with regard to building usage and style in writing

PREPARING FOR CONVENTIONS CLUBS

As with any unit of study, it is helpful to begin by "getting ready" to implement the unit. This ensures that the clubs run smoothly and that teachers and students feel ready for the exciting work ahead. We suggest getting ready for conventions clubs by gathering materials and envisioning how the work will go.

Gathering Materials

Conventions clubs, like all stand-alone clubs, will employ the materials you are currently using in writing workshop and add a layer of novel, new materials. Figure 8.1 shows the new materials for this type of club.

Figure 8.1
Writer's Notebooks with
Conventions Sections

Figure 8.2
Conventions
Anchor Charts

Figure 8.3
Children's Literature to Help Teach Conventions

Capitalization, Spelling, and Punctuation	Grammar and Parts of Speech
• *The Case of the Incapacitated Capitals* by Robin Pulver	• *The Great Grammar Book* by Kate Petty
• *Silent Letters Loud and Clear* by Robin Pulver	• *The Great Dictionary Caper* by Judy Sierra
• *Punctuation: The Write Stuff!* by Mary Budzir	• *Nouns and Verbs Have a Field Day* by Robin Pulver
• *Perfect (Pop-up) Punctuation Book* by Kate Petty	• *Merry-Go-Round: A Book About Nouns* by Ruth Heller
• *Whatever Says Mark: Knowing and Using Punctuation* by Terry Lee Collins	• *A Mink, a Fink, a Skating Rink: What Is a Noun?* by Brian P. Cleary
• *Eats, Shoots & Leaves: The Zero Tolerance Approach to Punctuation* by Lynne Truss	• *I and You and Don't Forget Who: What Is a Pronoun?* by Brian P. Cleary
• *Twenty-Odd Ducks: Why, Every Punctuation Mark Counts!* by Lynne Truss	• *If You Were a Pronoun* by Nancy Loewen
• *The Girl's Like Spaghetti: Why, You Can't Manage Without Apostrophes!* by Lynne Truss	• *To Root, to Toot, to Parachute: What Is a Verb?* by Brian P. Cleary
• *Punctuation Takes a Vacation* by Robin Pulver	• *Slide and Slurp, Scratch and Burp: More About Verbs* by Brian P. Cleary
• *The Punctuation Station* by Brian P. Cleary	• *Kites Sail High: A Book About Verbs* by Ruth Heller
• *Punctuation Celebration* by Elsa Knight Bruno	• *It's Hard to Be a Verb!* by Julia Cook
• *Exclamation Mark* by Amy Krouse Rosenthal	• *Under, Over, by the Clover: What Is a Preposition?* by Brian P. Cleary
• *Exclamation Points Say Wow* by Michael Dahl	• *Hairy, Scary, Ordinary: What Is an Adjective?* by Brian P. Cleary
• *Greedy Apostrophe: A Cautionary Tale* by Jan Carr	• *If You Were an Adjective* by Michael Dahl
• *If You Were an Apostrophe* by Shelly Lyons	• *A Is for Angry: An Animal and Adjective Alphabet* by Sandra Boynton
• *Alphie the Apostrophe* by Moira Rose Donohue	• *Dearly, Nearly, Insincerely: What Is an Adverb?* by Brian P. Cleary
• *Little i* by Michael Hall	• *Fantastic! Wow! and Unreal!: A Book About Interjections and Conjunctions* by Ruth Heller
• *Semicolons, Cupcakes, and Cucumbers* by Steve Newberry	• *Fortunately* by Remy Charlip
	• *Monkey Business* by Wallace Edwards

For conventions clubs, we use a club station model and want to provide other conventions tools at the stations, including:

1. **Mentor Sentences Written on Sentence Strips.** See Figure 8.6 for a list of our favorite mentor sentences.

2. **Grammar Tools.** These can be varied by unit and development of the writer, but some of our favorites include personal word walls, transitional word lists, grammar reference books, children's literature about writing conventions (Figure 8.3), and white boards for sentence try-its, to name a few.

Envisioning How the Work Will Go

Another way we get ready for conventions clubs is to engage in both a teacher assessment and a student self-assessment. These activities are integral to the start of this club because the clubs are based on strengths and next-step goals.

If you are working on your own, we suggest you use a piece of low-stakes student writing—from a notebook or an early draft—that represents what the writer habitually does. Place the student writing beside the following questions using Figure 8.4, the Conventions Assessment Tool:

1. Evaluate the following six dimensions of conventions. Indicate whether the writer uses the following according to the scale: seldom (S), some of the time (ST), most of the time (MT).

2. What misalignments do we see? Does the writer have a strength in some skills but surprising weakness in others?

3. When asked to reread and self-correct, what percentage of errors can the writer find?

Figure 8.4
The Conventions Assessment Tool

Spelling	Capitali-zation	End Punc-tuation	Pausing Punctua-tion	Other Punctua-tion	Sentence Structure

Question 3 may be difficult to answer by examining only one piece of writing. Feel free to think back or look back to other writing samples to determine how the writer does with self-correction and whether a tool is helpful in this endeavor. When using this tool, create a list of common needs for the class.

Another useful tool in examining student writing more collectively is the Protocol for Examining Student Work in Figure 8.5. When using this document with teachers, we often ask them to bring an on-demand piece of writing composed in a single sitting. This way, we can compare apples to apples and envision how we can inform the next unit of study.

It is helpful to examine student writing with colleagues and even trade writing samples to get their perspective. We often choose to "thin slice" out only one or two elements of conventions in any one sitting. This way, we can be focused and synthesize what we notice quickly. We have done this work many times with teachers and are able to notice and note much about student writing in a forty-five-minute planning period!

In addition to determining students' needs, it is important to check in with state and local standards. Consider the following questions:

- What conventions are students expected to master by the end of the year?

- What conventions are students expected to have exposure to by the end of the year?

- What are the expectations for the usage of these conventions across the year? Are there quarterly or trimester benchmarks?

Figure 8.5
Sample Protocol for Examining Student Work

After assessing students' needs and examining standards, teachers should gather texts and imagine the teaching possibilities around them. What texts demonstrate the conventions students should emulate? With regard to conventions, what does this author do especially well? Is this author someone who the students will gravitate toward and say, "I can do that, too!" What can this author teach the students to do better?

When Will Conventions Clubs Happen?

In Chapter 2, we provided options for how writing clubs can fit into the existing fabric of writing time. As we explained, clubs can happen in two ways: as a complement to another unit of study (integrated and threaded throughout) or as a stand-alone unit. Conventions clubs are the perfect stand-alone unit of study. They are joyful, purposeful, and very timely—typically two to three weeks. Although we have presented conventions clubs as stand-alone units, they also work great as a complement unit. See Figures 1.4 and 1.5 for two examples of conventions clubs within a year of writing instruction.

Teaching Points to Consider

When planning for conventions clubs, teachers often turn to favorite texts and study the authors' use of conventions. How did they use punctuation in meaningful ways? How do their choices lend voice to their writing? What can they teach students? Figure 8.6 on pages 156–157 shows some of our favorite texts and mentor sentences.

CLUB TIME

Conventions clubs may be new and even a bit scary, but if you give them a try, you will see the value and benefit of allowing students to play with language in a collaborative setting!

Part One: Forming and Launching Clubs

Forming and launching conventions clubs should mirror the launch of any stand-alone club. Therefore, you want to bring this club to students in a joyful and exciting way. You may choose to launch the club during a morning meeting, or you may choose to make the launch and the self-assessment part of the first minilesson. Either way, consider the moves

Figure 8.6
Mentor Sentences

Title and Author	Mentor Sentences	What Convention Can This Author Teach Other Writers?
The Day You Begin, Jacqueline Woodson	*There will be times when the world feels like a place that you're standing all the way outside of . . .*	Use of ellipses
Two Bobbies: A True Story of Hurricane Katrina, Friendship, and Survival, Kirby Larson and Mary Nethery	*Were Bobbi and Bob Cat chased away from any scraps they might have found?*	End punctuation: use of a question mark
	Together again at last!	End punctuation: use of an exclamation mark
Malala: A Brave Girl from Pakistan, Jeanette Winter	*Slowly, Malala wakes from the nightmare.*	Comma after an introductory phrase
14 Cows for America, Carmen Agra Deedy	*As Kimeli nears his village, he watches a herd of bull giraffes cross the open grassland.*	Complex sentence with introductory clause at the beginning of the sentence.
	He greets them with a gentle touch on the head, a warrior's blessing.	Complex sentence with a clause at the end of the sentence
Amazing Grace, Mary Hoffman	*After she had heard them, and sometimes while they were still going on, Grace would act them out.*	Use of commas in a complex sentence around an appositive phrase that adds detail to the sentence (telling more about who or when)
All About Rattlesnakes, Jim Arnosky	*All rattlesnakes have keeled scales, but not all snakes with keeled scales are rattlesnakes.*	Compound sentence joining two sentences using a coordinating conjunction and a comma
A Young Patriot: The American Revolution as Experienced by One Boy, Jim Murphy	*They were no longer the enemy; they were prisoners of war.*	Compound sentence combining two sentences without a conjunction

Title and Author	Mentor Sentences	What Convention Can This Author Teach Other Writers?
Frogs, Nic Bishop	*Frogs, for example, do not have rib bones.*	Sentence variety (inserting the "for example" inside the sentence)
Pink and Say, Patricia Polacco	*"You can call me say," I said.*	Punctuating dialogue with dialogue tag at end
	"Then you have been all alone here?" Pinkus asked his mother.	Punctuating dialogue when using a question.
The House on Mango Street, Sandra Cisneros, "Papa Who Wakes Up Tired in the Dark"	*My Papa, his thick hands and thick shoes, who wakes up tired in the dark, who combs his hair with water, drinks his coffee, and is gone before we wake, today is sitting on my bed.*	Serial comma
Amelia and Eleanor Go for a Ride, Pam Muñoz Ryan	*She carefully folded a gift for Eleanor—a silk scarf that matched her own.*	Use of an em dash to separate a dependent clause in a complex sentence (instead of a comma)

that Patty made in the following anecdote as she launched conventions clubs with a sixth-grade team.

> **Teacher:** Friends, I know that you have loved the writing club work that you have done this year, and I want to bring to you a new club opportunity. I can see some excitement in your faces, and before you change that excitement to a frown, I want to let you know that the clubs we are going to be doing are not like other, typical clubs. We are going to be starting conventions clubs. And before you start to groan, let me assure you that these types of clubs will be just as exciting and fun as the other clubs you have participated in this year.

Self-Assessment

In addition to assessing students in preparing for the unit, after you have announced the kind of clubs students will be participating in, ask students to self-assess and use the information they provide to help you form clubs. One way we ask students to self-assess is to use a simple form such as the one in Figure 8.7.

Figure 8.7
Conventions Self-Assessment

Conventions Self-Assessment	
Which element of conventions do you feel you are strong at? Check all that apply.	1. Spelling 2. Capitalization 3. Ending punctuation (. ! ?) 4. Pausing punctuation (, ; : — . . .) 5. Other punctuation (' " ") 6. Writing complete and correct sentences
What element of conventions feels challenging? Check all that apply.	1. Spelling 2. Capitalization 3. Ending punctuation (. ! ?) 4. Pausing punctuation (, ; : — . . .) 5. Other punctuation (' " ") 6. Writing complete and correct sentences
How do I feel about editing my own work?	
How do I feel about editing another student's work?	
What tools help me to write conventionally so others can read? Check all that apply.	1. Checklist 2. Mentor Sentence 3. Personal Word Wall 4. Other _____
What is a conventions goal that I have?	

The easiest way to form clubs is to engage in the student and teacher assessments and move into clubs based on what you see and what your students say. You might:

1. Ask students to engage in the self-assessment activity in Figure 8.7 and jigsaw share in pairs with a couple of different partnerships. Although the share is jigsaw format (each writer sharing something different from the first four reflection questions), all students share their conventions goal. Students note similarities and differences in their conventions strengths and goals. Partners then consider these similarities and differences and choose three other possible partner groups to work with. Their choices can be based on similar strengths, similar goals, different strengths that match another pair's goals, or any other method. The key is for students to be cognizant of their strengths and what they most hope to get out of the conventions clubs. Teachers can then pair two partnerships based on student input.

2. Ask students to engage in the reflection activity in Figure 8.7 and conduct a gallery walk of the information. Students silently go along and note the similarities and differences between themselves and other writers. They consider what conventions strengths they and their peers have, as well as goals for improving their writing conventions. Students then submit a reflection explaining how they would like to be grouped in a club—with students who have the same goal or with students who have the same strengths. Teachers then create clubs based on student requests.

Launching Clubs

It was midyear when sixth-grade teachers April and Briana sat down with Patty to discuss the writing work that students had been doing thus far. They requested that "conventions" be the topic of the professional development session, because they were concerned that the conventions teaching that they had been doing was not sticking in ways they wanted. This sentiment is a familiar one to us—we felt this about our own students all too often.

Patty was going to model not only a conventions lesson but a conventions concept, one that would stand on the shoulders of all of the collaboration work that had happened thus far that year.

Students already had writing partners and had been working with their current partners for a few weeks as they were finishing up their most recent unit of study. Students were working to edit the final drafts of their literary essays. Patty asked the teachers for a resource they were using so that she could implement the lesson. They shared the checklist shown in Figure 8.8.

Patty then introduced the teachers to the concept of conventions clubs and used her demo lesson to introduce the concept. In her lesson, she did two things: "thin sliced" the checklist into small chunks, and set up stations within the room. Figure 8.9 shows the revised checklist.

What she highlighted is what students would focus on in the upcoming editing round. With regard to how the editing happened, Patty set up

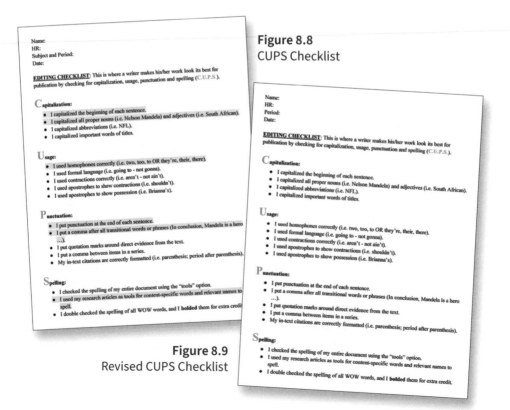

Figure 8.8
CUPS Checklist

Figure 8.9
Revised CUPS Checklist

conventions stations that would become the precursor to a conventions club model in the unit. The stations are shown in Figure 8.10.

Patty then conducted a minilesson where she introduced the concept and the centers and modeled taking the mentor text essay to each station. Partners then quickly paired with other partner groups and went off to the editing stations. At the wrap-up of the day's workshop, Patty and April asked students to reflect on the station model: What worked? What else would they need to edit in stations/centers going forward? How did they feel about the station resources? Too much? Too little? Something different needed? This conversation and reflection can then enable students to move into a conventions club unit.

Figure 8.10
Depiction of Conventions Stations

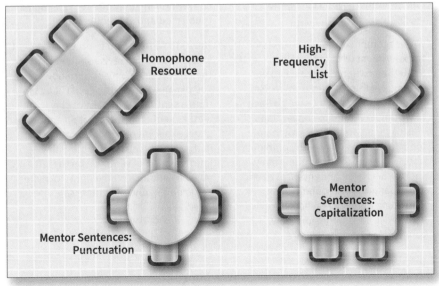

Part Two: Lessons

Conventions clubs are opportunities to illuminate the conventions of writing in powerful and purposeful ways. Note that *how* you teach conventions, and the ways in which you engage students purposefully and playfully, matters just as much as *what* you teach. Conventions club lessons follow a similar teaching arc to any unit of study, as shown in Figure 8.11: immersion and identification of the upcoming learning, practice and experimentation, publishing and reflection.

Figure 8.11
What to Teach: The Arc of Conventions Lessons

Lesson	How to Teach/Tool
Writers reflect on their strengths and set goals based on what they want to work on. This is true for all areas of writing—even conventions. Today, I am going to teach you how to reflect on your convention use and set goals so that we can begin writing conventions clubs!	Provide students with conventions self-assessment tool (see Figure 8.7 for sample student self-assessment).
Engage in immersion around conventions. Ask students questions to encourage them to hypothesize and build theories around convention usage.	Use a single-focus model to immerse students in one convention at a time. Allow time to notice, name, and note the convention in many different examples (published and student-created).
Writers compose and revise texts to experiment with conventions. Sometimes when we go back to our writing, we think we do so to revise the craft. But sometimes we go back to writing to attend to conventions. This could mean that we switch up the punctuation, play with combining phrases or sentences to make new shorter or longer sentences, or even move paragraphs around. Today I am going to teach you how to revise a sentence considering our new conventions knowledge.	Have students return to previously written entries to revise sentences with their newfound conventions knowledge. You can use the strategies of Lift a Line (find a sentence you want to play with, lift that sentence and put it on another page, experiment with that convention in that sentence) or a double-entry journal (original sentence on the left, revised sentence on the right) to invite engagement and playfulness.

Lesson	How to Teach/Tool
Writers use tools such as checklists to compose or edit a piece of writing with their new conventions knowledge.	See sample editing checklists in Figures 8.13a and 8.13b.
Writers reflect on what they have learned about conventions and how their writing has been enhanced by this new knowledge.	See sample student reflection in Figure 8.7.

Figure 8.12
How to Teach: Seven Daily Pedagogical Practices

Seven Daily Pedagogical Practices

1. Practice editing and writing conventionally in an ongoing, everyday manner. Use strategies like daily edit (time at the end of each writing workshop to reread for clarity and conventions) or express editing (Anderson 2005) to build automaticity and engagement with conventional writing.

2. Lift a line from literature, generalize some principles, and apply them to writing. Tuck these ten-minute exercises a few times into each unit of study.

3. Lift a sentence from literature and leave out one piece of the punctuation you've taught or make one usage error and have students correct. These make great pre-workshop activities to be done before the minilesson begins.

4. Examine your students' writing, and find common mistakes they make. Use this knowledge to inform the conventions/editing minilessons in each unit of study. We usually say something such as, *I notice that you are writing some really robust complex and compound sentences. However, I also notice that you are having a hard time writing these so others can read them. Let's take a look at a complex sentence and see if we can look at how to . . .*

5. Use the double journal entry format for daily editing and conventions practice. Ask students to imitate a convention (a comma in a series, an appositive phrase, transition at the beginning or in the middle of a sentence, etc.) and talk about its uses—try-it writing.

6. Find an example of a rule or convention from a mentor text and make it a mentor sentence. See Figure 8.6 for some sample mentor sentences. Put mentor sentences on sentence strips, and have these sentence strips available as tools for students to use on anchor charts, in Google Classroom, or as a tool in their writer's notebooks. Ask students to write like these sentences.

7. Edit in stations. Each station represents a different element you want students to examine in their own writing (e.g., spelling station, punctuation station, capitalization station). Have students edit just for those elements in each station. Rotate to move through your editing checklist.

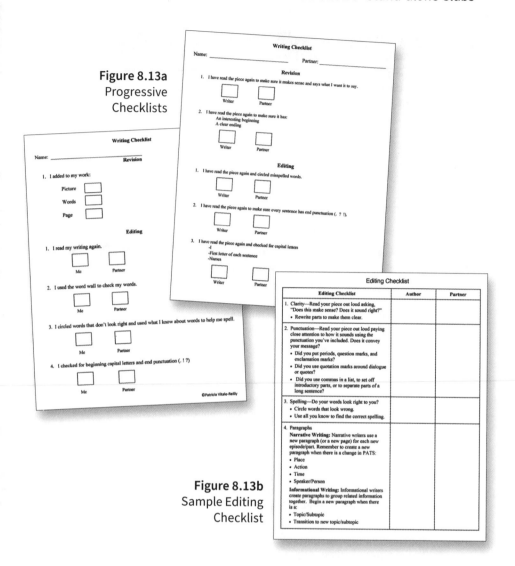

Figure 8.13a
Progressive
Checklists

Figure 8.13b
Sample Editing
Checklist

Part Three: Clubbing Through the Conventions Clubs

Here is one way conventions club can go. This example is from a sixth-grade classroom. Students already participated in the self-assessment activities, and clubs were formed *before* the first minilesson. In addition to minilessons about conventions, these units included minilessons on writing process and collaboration. Please keep in mind that if the club meeting box is empty, there is no meeting during writing. If the box states writing time in the box, students are writing as usual in workshop.

Figure 8.14
Conventions Clubs Unit

Grade: 6	Unit: Conventions Clubs		Timeframe: Three Weeks	
	Day 1:	**Day 2:**	**Day 3:**	**Day 4:**	**Day 5:**

	Day 1:	**Day 2:**	**Day 3:**	**Day 4:**	**Day 5:**
Minilesson	Reading like a conventional writer: rereading our favorite texts to notice, name, and note the use of conventions (capitalization and font types, punctuation, parts of speech, vivid verbs, striking adjectives)	Express edit: reread your writing for one or two things	Comma bootcamp: introductory phrases	Comma bootcamp: the serial comma	Comma bootcamp: commas in appositive phrases
Club Meeting			Discuss theories around where introductory commas are used and why		What is an appositive, and why would I use them?
Writing and Conferring	Immersion and noticing conventions as a club	Notebook entry writing: students have the last five to seven minutes to express edit.	Notebook entry writing	Notebook entry writing: students have the last five to seven minutes to express edit for serial commas and introductory commas.	Notebook entry writing
Wrap-Up	Notice, Name, and Note chart	Clubs share their express edits and their reflections on the strategy.	Check in: How is writing going? Use any introductory commas?	Make someone famous: share an entry with comma usage.	Comma experts: set up an expert board with examples from comma expert writing.

Figure 8.14 (continued)   Conventions Clubs Unit

	Day 6:	Day 7:	Day 8:	Day 9:	Day 10:
Minilesson	Double-entry journal writing to revise sentences	Spelling tools: how to use them in everyday writing	Five-minute review of the Notice, Name, and Note protocol with new mentor sentences—awesome adjectives	Sentence bootcamp: how to make a compound sentence	Sentence bootcamp: how to make complex sentences that don't feel too complex!
Club Meeting			Study mentor texts: notice and name the use of adjectives		
Writing and Conferring	Find previously written sentences (or a whole entry) and place them on the left-hand side of a page; rewrite sentences with your newfound conventions prowess!	Writing time and midworkshop: notebook entry writing; giving a glow and a grow to fellow writers in our club	Polishing a notebook entry with newfound conventions knowledge: meet with clubs flexibly	Notebook writing of a new entry or of an entry consisting of lines lifted and revised to be powerful compound sentences	Writing time and midworkshop: notebook entry writing; Quaker share of simple to complex sentences
Wrap-Up	Clubs meet to share revised sentences.	Wrap-up/club time: provide feedback on entries/drafts written using the inspiration and techniques learned.	Club gallery walk	Status of the Class (Atwell, 1987): Where are you, and where are you going next?	Clubs continue to study mentor sentences of compound and complex sentences.

	Day 11:	Day 12:	Day 13:	Day 14:	Day 15:
Minilesson	Sentence bootcamp: varying simple, compound, and complex sentences	Exploring the dramatic pause: colons, semicolons, and ellipses	Editing in stations: How do we support each other in clubs as we cycle through stations to edit for punctuation, capitalization, usage, and spelling?	Publishing using our conventions club checklist	Writing celebration and club reflection
Club Meeting		Studying authors' use of pausing punctuation in mentor sentences and texts		*No official club time. Clubs may choose to meet.*	
Writing and Conferring	Notebook entry writing	Playing around with the pause	Revision and editing stations	Polishing our pieces	
Wrap-Up	Sitting in the Chair protocol, whole group	Choosing another piece to polish	Feedback on revision and editing	Preparing for celebration	

LIFE AFTER CONVENTIONS CLUBS

We have found that conventions clubs leave students with a sense of joy and playfulness in writing! Students are empowered by the tools they use, the ability to play with language, and the experience of being both mentor and mentee. We therefore suggest that regardless of where you go next, you continue this thread in other units. In particular:

- Continue to teach conventions in these authentic and playful ways! Don't revert to traditional grammar lessons—keep up the work with mentor sentences, express editing, double-page journals, and student experts!

- Keep the conventions clubbing alive! Envision how you can use conventions clubs as a complement unit, or even just envision that all future editing will be in the stations model.

- Keep low-stakes writing alive. This unit was grounded in lots of try-its and experimentation. Writers really flourish when they have these opportunities to work on their writing outside of publishing cycles. Commit to enough low-stakes writing in each unit of study going forward.

References

Anderson, Jeff. 2005. *Mechanically Inclined*. Portland, ME: Stenhouse.

Atwell, Nancie. 1987. *In the Middle: New Understandings about Writing, Reading, and Learning*. Portsmouth, NH: Heinemann.

Bishop, Rudine Sims. 1990. "Mirrors, Windows, and Sliding Glass Doors." In *Perspectives: Choosing and Using Books for the Classroom*. Volume 6, no. 3.

Calkins, Lucy. 1994. *The Art of Teaching Writing*. Portsmouth, NH: Heinemann.

Calkins, Lucy, and Colleen Gillette. 2006. *Breathing Life into Essays*. Portsmouth, NH: Heinemann.

Calkins, Lucy, Kelly Hohne, and Audra Robb. 2013. *Writing Pathways: Performance Assessments and Learning Progressions*. Portsmouth, NH: Heinemann.

Calkins, Lucy, and Alexandra Marron. 2013. *Narrative Craft*. Portsmouth, NH: Heinemann.

Calkins, Lucy, and Marjorie Martinelli. 2006. *Launching the Writing Workshop*. Portsmouth, NH: Heinemann.

Coppola, Shawna. 2021. "How to Inspire Students to Write Using Comics and Graphic Novels." grassrootsworkshops.com. Accessed June 24, 2021.

Cruz, M. Colleen. 2004. *Independent Writing: One Teacher—Thirty-Two Needs, Topics, and Plans*. Portsmouth, NH: Heinemann.

Eickholdt, Lisa. 2015. *Learning from Classmates: Using Students' Writing as Mentor Texts*. Portsmouth, NH: Heinemann.

Fletcher, Ralph. 2017. *Joy Write: Cultivating High-Impact, Low-Stakes Writing*. Portsmouth, NH: Heinemann.

Gambrell, Linda. 1996. *Lively Discussions! Fostering Engaged Reading*. Newark, DE: International Literacy Association.

Goodman, Yetta. 1985. "Kid Watching: Observing Children in the Classroom." In *Observing the Language Learner,* ed. A. Jaggar and M. T. Smith-Burke (9–18). Newark, DE: International Reading Association.

Graves, Donald. 1983. *Writing: Teachers and Children at Work.* Portsmouth, NH: Heinemann.

Graves, Donald, and Jane Hansen. 1983. "The Author's Chair." *Language Arts* 60 (2):176–183.

Hattie, John. 2009. *Visible Learning: A Synthesis of Over 800 Meta-Analyses Relating to Achievement.* New York: Routledge.

Lamott, Anne. 1995. *Bird by Bird: Some Instructions on Writing and Life.* New York: Pantheon Books.

Miller, Donalyn. 2014. "No More Language Arts and Crafts." https://bookwhisperer.com/2014/09/07/.

Muhtaris, Katie, and Kristin Ziemke. 2015. *Amplify: Digital Teaching and Learning in the K–6 Classroom.* Portsmouth, NH: Heinemann.

Murray, Donald. 1972. "Teaching Writing as a Process Not Product." *The Leaflet* 71 (3):11–14.

———. 1985. *A Writer Teaches Writing.* 2nd ed. Boston: Houghton Mifflin.

———. 1989. *Expecting the Unexpected: Teaching Myself—and Others—To Read and Write.* Portsmouth, NH: Heinemann.

Newkirk, Thomas, and Penny Kittle. 2013. *Children Want to Write: Donald Graves and the Revolution in Children's Writing.* Portsmouth, NH: Heinemann.

New York State Education Department. 2017. "New York State Next Generation English Language Arts Learning Standards." Accessed June 20, 2021. http://www.nysed.gov/common/nysed/files/programs/curriculum-instruction/nys-next-generation-ela-standards.pdf.

Palmisano, Samuel J. 2010. "Capitalizing on Complexity." CEO survey. January 1. Accessed July 28, 2014. www.inspireimagineinnovate.com/PDF/Capitalizing-on-Complexity-IBM-Study.pdf.

Petersen, Ralph. 1992. *Life in a Crowded Place: Making a Learning Community.* Portsmouth, NH: Heinemann.

Portalupi, JoAnn, and Ralph Fletcher. 2004. *Teaching the Qualities of Writing.* Portsmouth, NH: Heinemann.

Puentedura, Ruben R. 2014. "SAMR And TPCK: A Hands-On Approach to Classroom Practice." http://www.hippasus.com/rrpweblog/archives/2014/12/11/SAMRandTPCK_HandsOnApproachClassroomPractice.pdf.

Ray, Katie Wood. 1999. *Wondrous Words: Writers and Writing in the Elementary Classroom*. Urbana, IL: National Council of Teachers of English.

————. 2006. *Study Driven: A Framework for Planning Units of Study in the Writing Workshop*. Portsmouth, NH: Heinemann.

Ray, Katie Wood, and Lester Laminack. 2001. *Writing Workshop: Working Through the Hard Parts (and They're All Hard Parts)*. Urbana, IL: National Council of Teachers of English.

Routman, Regie. 1999. *Conversations: Strategies for Teaching, Learning and Evaluating*. Portsmouth, NH: Heinemann.

Vitale-Reilly, Patricia. 2015. *Engaging Every Learner: Classroom Principles, Strategies, and Tools*. Portsmouth, NH: Heinemann.

————. 2017. *Supporting Struggling Learners: 50 Instructional Moves for the Classroom Teacher*. Portsmouth, NH: Heinemann.

Vygotsky, L. S. 1978. *Mind in Society: The Development of Higher Psychological Processes*. Cambridge, MA: Harvard University Press.

Children's Literature Bibliography

Arnosky, Jim. 2002. *All About Rattlesnakes*. New York: Scholastic.

Bishop, Nic. 2008. *Frogs*. New York: Scholastic Nonfiction.

Black, Michael Ian. 2010. *A Pig Parade Is a Terrible Idea*. New York: Simon & Schuster Books for Young Readers.

Boelts, Maribeth, and Noah Jones. 2009. *Those Shoes*. Somerville, MA: Candlewick.

Boynton, Sandra. 2016. *A Is for Angry: An Animal and Adjective Alphabet*. St. Louis, MO: Turtleback Books.

Brinkloe, Julie. 1986. *Fireflies*. New York: Aladdin Books.

Brown, L. Mahogany, with Elizabeth Acevedo and Olivia Gatwood. 2020. *Woke: A Young Poet's Call to Justice*. New York: Roaring Brook.

Brown, Peter. 2009. *The Curious Garden*. New York: Little, Brown Books for Young Readers.

———. 2010. *Flight of the Dodo*. New York: Little, Brown Books for Young Readers.

———. 2011. *You Will Be My Friend!* New York: Little, Brown Books for Young Readers.

———. 2013. *Mr. Tiger Goes Wild*. New York: Little, Brown Books for Young Readers.

———. 2016. *The Wild Robot*. New York: Little, Brown Books for Young Readers.

———. 2018. *The Wild Robot Escapes*. New York: Little, Brown Books for Young Readers.

Bruno, Elsa Knight. 2012. *Punctuation Celebration*. New York: Square Fish Books.

Bryant, Kobe. 2015. "Dear Basketball." *The Player's Tribune.*

Budzir, Mary. 2017. *Punctuation: The Write Stuff!* New York: Kingfisher Children's Books.

Bunting, Eve. 1992. *The Wall.* New York: Clarion Books.

———. 1993. *Fly Away Home.* New York: Clarion Books.

———. 1996. *Secret Place.* New York: Clarion Books.

———. 1996. *Train to Somewhere.* New York: Clarion Books

———. 1997. *A Day's Work.* New York: Clarion Books.

———. 1999. *Smoky Night.* Boston, MA: HMH Books for Young Readers.

———. 2001. *Dandelions.* Boston, MA: HMH Books for Young Readers.

Carr, Jan. 2009. *Greedy Apostrophe: A Cautionary Tale.* New York: Holiday House.

Charlip, Remy. 1993. *Fortunately.* New York: Aladdin Books.

Cisneros, Sandra. 1991. *The House on Mango Street.* New York: Vintage.

———. 1992. *Woman Hollering Creek: And Other Stories.* New York: Vintage.

Cleary, Brian P. 1999. *A Mink, a Fink, a Skating Rink: What Is a Noun?* Minneapolis, MN: Millbrook.

———. 2001. *Hairy, Scary, Ordinary: What Is an Adjective?.* Minneapolis, MN: Millbrook.

———. 2001. *To Root, to Toot, to Parachute: What Is a Verb?* Minneapolis, MN: Carolrhoda Books.

———. 2003. *Under, Over, by the Clover: What Is a Preposition?* Minneapolis, MN: Millbrook.

———. 2005. *Dearly, Nearly, Insincerely: What Is an Adverb?* Minneapolis, MN: Millbrook.

———. 2006. *I and You and Don't Forget Who: What Is a Pronoun?* Minneapolis, MN: Millbrook.

———. 2009. *Slide and Slurp, Scratch and Burp: More About Verbs.* Minneapolis, MN: Millbrook.

———. 2010. *The Punctuation Station.* Minneapolis, MN: Millbrook.

Collins, Terry Lee. 2013. *Whatever Says Mark: Knowing and Using Punctuation.* Bloomington, MN: Picture Window Books.

Cook, Julia. 2008. *It's Hard to Be a Verb.* Chattanooga, TN: National Center for Youth Issues.

Cornwell, Gaia. 2020. *Jabari Jumps*. Somerville, MA: Candlewick.

Dahl, Michael. 2006. *If You Were an Adjective*. Bloomington, MN: Picture Window Books.

———. 2019. *Exclamation Points Say Wow*. Bloomington, MN: Picture Window Books.

Deedy, Carmen Agra. 1994. *The Library Dragon*. Atlanta, GA: Peachtree.

———. 1995. *Growing Up Cuban in Decatur, Georgia*. Atlanta, GA: Peachtree.

———. 1995. *The Last Dance*. Atlanta, GA: Peachtree.

———. 2001. *The Yellow Star: The Legend of King Christian X of Denmark*. Atlanta, GA: Peachtree.

———. 2007. *Martina the Beautiful Cockroach*. Atlanta, GA: Peachtree.

———. 2011. *The Cheshire Cheese Cat: A Dickens of a Tale*. Atlanta, GA: Peachtree.

———. 2016. *14 Cows for America*. Atlanta, GA: Peachtree.

de la Peña, Matt. 2005. *Ball Don't Lie*. New York: Delacorte.

———. 2008. *Mexican White Boy*. New York: Delacorte.

———. 2009. *We Were Here*. New York: Delacorte.

———. 2013. *A Nation's Hope: The Story of Boxing Legend Joe Louis*. New York: Puffin Books.

———. 2013. *Curse of the Ancients*. Infinity Ring #4. New York: Scholastic.

———. 2015. *Last Stop on Market Street*. New York: G.P. Putnam's Sons Books for Young Readers.

———. 2016. *Eternity*. Infinity Ring #8. New York: Scholastic.

———. 2018. *Carmela Full of Wishes*. New York: G.P. Putnam's Sons Books for Young Readers.

———. 2018. *Love*. New York: G.P. Putnam's Sons Books for Young Readers.

———. 2019. *Superman: Dawnbreaker*. New York: Random House Books for Young Readers.

———. 2021. *Milo Imagines the World*. New York: G.P. Putnam's Sons Books for Young Readers.

Donahue, Moira Rose. 2010. *Alphie the Apostrophe*. Park Ridge, IL: Albert Whitman.

Edwards, Wallace. 2008. *Monkey Business*. Toronto, Canada: Kids Can Press.

Evans, Shira. 2018. *National Geographic Readers: Tadpole to Frog.* Washington, DC: National Geographic Kids.

Frazee, Marla. 2006. *Roller Coaster.* Boston, MA: HMH Books for Young Readers.

Garza Lomas, Carmen. 2005. *Family Pictures.* New York: Children's Book Press.

Gibbons, Gail. 2019. *Hurricanes.* New York: Holiday House.

Giovanni, Nikki. 2018. *I Am Loved.* New York: Atheneum Books.

Greenfield, Eloise. 1986. *Honey, I Love and Other Love Poems.* New York: HarperCollins.

———. 1993. *Childtimes: A Three-Generation Memoir.* New York: HarperCollins.

———. 1998. *For the Love of the Game: Michael Jordan and Me.* New York: HarperCollins.

———. 2010. *The Great Migration: Journey to the North.* New York: HarperCollins.

———. 2016. *In the Land of Words: New and Selected Poems.* New York: HarperCollins.

Hall, Michael. 2017. *Little i.* New York: Greenwillow.

Heller, Ruth. 1998. *Kites Sail High: A Book About Verbs.* London: Puffin Books.

———. 1998. *Merry-Go-Round: A Book About Nouns.* London: Puffin Books.

———. 2000. *Fantastic! Wow! And Unreal!: A Book About Interjections and Conjunctions.* London: Puffin Books.

Hoffman, Mary. 1991. *Amazing Grace.* New York: Dial Books for Young Readers.

Hudson, Wade, and Cheryl Willis Hudson. 2019. *We Rise We Resist We Raise Our Voices.* New York: Yearling.

Hughes, Langston. 1996. *The Dream Keeper and Other Poems.* New York: Knopf.

Jenkins, Steve. 2008. *What Do You Do with a Tail Like This?* Boston, MA: HMH Books for Young Readers.

———. 2011. *Actual Size.* Boston, MA: HMH Books for Young Readers.

———. 2014. *Creature Features: Twenty-Five Animals Explain Why They Look the Way They Do.* Boston, MA: HMH Books for Young Readers.

———. 2017. *Who Am I?: An Animal Guessing Game.* Boston, MA: HMH Books for Young Readers.

———. 2018. *Look at Me!: How to Attract Attention in the Animal World.* Boston, MA: HMH Books for Young Readers.

Johnson, Angela. 2007. *A Sweet Smell of Roses.* New York: Simon & Schuster Books for Young Readers.

Keats, Ezra Jack. 1964. *Whistle for Willie.* New York: Viking Books for Young Readers.

———. 1996. *The Snowy Day.* New York: Viking Books for Young Readers.

———. 1998. *A Letter to Amy.* New York: Viking Books for Young Readers.

———. 1998. *Goggles!* London: Puffin Books.

———. 1998. *Peter's Chair.* London: Puffin Books.

———. 1999. *Apt. 3.* London: Puffin Books.

———. 2001. *Pet Show.* London: Puffin Books.

Kerascot. 2018. *I Walk with Vanessa: A Story About a Simple Act of Kindness.* Canada: Schwartz & Wade.

Larson, Kirby, and Mary Netherey. 2008. *Two Bobbies: A True Story of Hurricane Katrina, Friendship, and Survival.* New York: Walker & Company.

Layne, Steven L. 2003. *My Brother Dan's Delicious.* New Orleans, LA: Pelican.

Loewen, Nancy. 2006. *If You Were a Pronoun.* Bloomington, MN: Picture Window Books.

Lowry, Lois. 2009. *Crow Call.* New York: Scholastic.

Ludwig, Trudy, and Patrice Barton. 2013. *The Invisible Boy.* New York: Knopf.

Lyons, Shelly. 2009. *If You Were an Apostrophe.* Bloomington, MN: Picture Window Books.

MacLachlan, Patricia. 2010. *Word After Word After Word.* New York: Katherine Tegen Books.

MacLachlan, Patricia, and Mike Wimmer. 1994. *All the Places to Love.* New York: HarperCollins.

McCloskey, Kevin. 2016. *The Real Poop on Pigeons! A Toon Book.* TOON Books.

Miller Zietlow, Pat. 2018. *Be Kind.* New York: Roaring Brook.

Morrison, Toni. 1999. *The Big Box (Jump at the Sun).* New York: Little, Brown Books for Young Readers.

Murphy, Jim. 1998. *A Young Patriot: The American Revolution as Experienced by One Boy.* New York: Clarion Books.

Newberry, Steve. 2017. *Semicolons, Cupcakes, and Cucumbers*. Seattle, WA: The Innovation Press.

O'Brien, Anne. 2018. *I'm New Here*. Watertown, MA: Charlesbridge Books.

Oh, Ellen. 2018. *Flying Lessons & Other Stories*. New York: Yearling.

Pearlman, Robb, and Eda Kaban. 2018. *Pink Is for Boys*. Philadelphia, PA: Running Press Kids.

Peirce, Lincoln. 2010–2016. The Big Nate series. New York: HarperCollins.

Penfold, Alexander, and Suzanne Kaufmann. 2018. *All Are Welcome*. New York: Penguin Random House.

Petty, Kate. 2006. *The Perfect Pop-Up Punctuation Book*. New York: Dutton Juvenile.

———. 2018. *The Great Grammar Book*. Somerville, MA: Candlewick.

Polacco, Patricia. 1994. *Pink and Say*. New York: Philomel Books.

———. 1997. *Thunder Cake*. London: Puffin Books.

———. 1998. *My Rotten Redheaded Older Brother*. New York: Simon & Schuster.

———. 1998. *The Bee Tree*. London: Puffin Books.

———. 2001. *The Keeping Quilt*. New York: Simon & Schuster.

———. 2012. *Thank You, Mr. Falker*. New York: Philomel Books.

Pulver, Robin. 2004. *Punctuation Takes a Vacation*. New York: Holiday House.

———. 2007. *Nouns and Verbs Have a Field Day*. New York: Holiday House.

———. 2010. *Silent Letters Loud and Clear*. New York: Holiday House.

———. 2013. *The Case of the Incapacitated Capitals*. New York: Holiday House.

Rosenthal, Amy Krouse. 2013. *Exclamation Mark*. New York: Scholastic.

Ryan, Pam Muñoz. 1999. *Amelia and Eleanor Go for a Ride*. New York: Scholastic.

Rylant, Cynthia. 1987–2005. The Henry and Mudge Series. New York: Simon Spotlight.

———. 1991. *Night in the Country*. New York: Atheneum Books.

———. 1993. *The Relatives Came*. New York: Aladdin Books.

———. 1993. *When I Was Young in the Mountains*. London: Puffin Books.

———. 2001. *The Great Gracie Chase: Stop That Dog!* New York: Blue Sky.

———. 2001. *Waiting to Waltz*. New York: Atheneum Books.

———. 2003. *The Wonderful Happens*. New York: Simon & Schuster.

———. 2004. *I Had Seen Castles*. Boston, MA: HMH Books for Young Readers.

———. 2006. *A Fine White Dust*. New York: Atheneum Books.

———. 2006. *The Van Gogh Cafe*. Boston, MA: HMH Books for Young Readers.

———. 2008. *In November*. Boston, MA: HMH Books for Young Readers.

———. 2011. *Every Living Thing*. New York: Atheneum Books.

———. 2016. *Best Wishes*. Somers, NY: Richard C. Owen.

———. 2018. *Cobble Street Cousins Complete Collection*. New York: Aladdin Books.

———. 2018. *Rosetown*. San Diego, CA: Beach Lane Books.

Say, Allen. 2008. *Grandfather's Journey*. Torrance, CA: Sandpiper Books.

Sierra, Judy. 2018. *The Great Dictionary Caper*. New York: Simon & Schuster.

Simon, Seymour. 2003. *The Moon*. New York: Simon & Schuster.

———. 2005. *Guts: Our Digestive System*. New York: HarperCollins.

———. 2007. *Spiders*. New York: HarperCollins.

———. 2009. *Dogs*. New York: HarperCollins.

———. 2014. The Einstein Anderson: Science Geek Series. New York: Scholastic.

———. 2019. *How to Talk to Your Computer*. New York: HarperCollins.

Stewart, Melissa. 2009. *National Geographic Readers: Snakes!*. Washington, DC: National Geographic Kids.

———. 2011. *National Geographic Readers: Deadliest Animals*. Washington, DC: National Geographic Kids.

Truss, Lynne. 2006. *Eats, Shoots & Leaves: The Zero Tolerance Approach to Punctuation*. New York: Avery.

———. 2007. *The Girl's Like Spaghetti: Why, You Can't Manage Without Apostrophes!* New York: G.P. Putnam's Sons Books for Young Readers.

———. 2008. *Twenty-Odd Ducks: Why, Every Punctuation Mark Counts!* New York: G.P. Putnam's Sons Books for Young Readers.

Winter, Jeanette. 2014. *Malala, a Brave Girl from Pakistan*. San Diego, CA: Beach Lane Books.

Wood, Brian. 2016. *Rebels: A Well-Regulated Militia*. Milwaukie, OR: Dark Horse Books.

Woodsen, Jacqueline. 1997. *We Had a Picnic This Sunday Past*. New York: Hyperion.

————. 2001. *The Other Side.* New York: G.P. Putnam's Sons Books for Young Readers.

————. 2002. *Last Summer with Maizon.* London: Puffin Books.

————. 2004. *Coming on Home Soon.* New York: G.P. Putnam's Sons Books for Young Readers.

————. 2005. *Show Way.* New York: G.P. Putnam's Sons Books for Young Readers.

————. 2010. *From the Notebooks of Melanin Sun.* London: Puffin Books.

————. 2010. *I Hadn't Meant to Tell You This.* London: Puffin Books.

————. 2012. *Each Kindness.* New York: Nancy Paulsen Books.

————. 2013. *Pecan Pie Baby.* London: Puffin Books.

————. 2013. *This Is the Rope: A Story from the Great Mitigation.* London: Puffin Books.

————. 2014. *Brown Girl Dreaming.* London: Puffin Books.

————. 2018. *Harbor Me.* New York: Nancy Paulsen Books.

————. 2019. *The Day You Begin.* New York: Nancy Paulsen Books.

Yolen, Jane. 1987. *Owl Moon.* New York: Philomel Books.

————. 1988. *The Devil's Arithmetic.* London: Puffin Books.

————. 1994. *Grandad Bill's Song.* New York: Philomel Books.

————. 1995. *Letting Swift River Go.* New York: Little, Brown Books for Young Readers.

————. 1996. *Encounter.* Boston, MA: HMH Books for Young Readers.

————. 2003. *Water Music.* Honesdale, PA: Wordsong.

————. 2014. How Do Dinosaurs (Five-Book Set). New York: Scholastic.

Index

NOTE: *f* = figure